HOPE
MEDICINE & HEALING

Francisco Contreras, MD
Daniel E. Kennedy, MC

Hope, Medicine & Healing
By Dr. Francisco Contreras & Daniel E. Kennedy
Published by Oasis of Hope Press
1685 Precision Park Lane, Suite L
San Diego, CA 92173
1-888-500-HOPE
Tel. (619) 428-0930
Fax. (619) 428-0994

Publisher & Editor: Daniel E. Kennedy
Researchers & Contributors: Jorge Barroso-Aranda, MD, PhD, Mark
McCarty, Leticia Wong, and Michael Wood.
Cover Design/Graphic Design/Formatting: Viviana Flores
Proof Readers: Michael Wood, Jorge Barroso-Aranda, MD, PhD,
Mark McCarty, Josue Barragan, and Estela Kennedy.

International Standard Book Number: 978-1-57946-009-9

This book is not intended to provide medical advice or to take the
place of medical advice and treatment from your personal physician.
Readers are advised to consult their own doctors or other qualified
health professionals regarding the treatment of their medical problems.
Neither the publisher nor the authors take any responsibility for any
possible consequences from any treatment, action or application of
medicine, supplement, herb or preparation to any person reading or
following information in this book. If readers are taking prescription
medications, again, they should consult with their physicians and not
take themselves off of medicines to start supplementations or a nutrition
program without the proper supervision of a physician.

Printed in the United States of America

Dedication

To you, the brave, it is my honor to walk this path with you.

Acknowledgements

This book is based largely on the research conducted by Jorge Barroso-Aranda, MD, PhD and Mark McCarty, which is published in their book *Integrative Regulatory Therapy: A Multi-Focal Approach to Cancer Control.* The Oasis of Hope director of emotional and spiritual life, Leticia Wong, PhD, also made important contributions to this book. Michael Wood did a phenomenal job of helping bring this book together and illustrating many of the concepts in ways that many can relate to. Steve Yount, from A. Larry Ross Communications, and Gaston Tessada of the Oasis of Hope, were valuable voices during the development of this book. It is much more readable because of their objective observations. Mary Bernal joyfully and faithfully supported the creative process and Viviana Flores used her talents of graphic design to help transmit an effective visual message. Thanks to Josue Barragan for adding his proofreading skills. We wish to personally thank each of our patients, whom we now call friends, who shared their victory over cancer stories in this book. These testimonies are what keep us going!

Note To The Reader

Hope, Medicine & Healing was written in the first person and expresses the opinions and experiences of either Dr. Francisco Contreras or Daniel E. Kennedy, or both, though no clarification is made. All testimonies submitted by the patients are included in this book with their consents.

About The Authors

Dr. Francisco Contreras serves as director, president, and chairman of the Oasis of Hope Hospital. A distinguished oncologist and surgeon, Contreras is renowned for combining conventional and alternative medical practices with emotional and spiritual support to provide patients with the most positive treatment experience possible. Oasis of Hope was founded by Contreras' father, Dr. Ernesto Contreras, Sr., in 1963 and since then the hospital has provided integrative cancer treatment for more than 100,000 patients.

After graduating with honors from medical school at the Autonomous University of Mexico in Toluca, Contreras specialized in surgical oncology at the University of Vienna in Austria, where he also graduated with honors.

Contreras has authored and co-authored several books concerning integrative therapy including *The Hope of Living Cancer Free, The Coming Cancer Cure, Fighting Cancer 20 Different Ways and Dismantling Cancer.*

Daniel E. Kennedy serves as chief executive officer of the Oasis of Hope Hospital. He is the grandson of Oasis of Hope founder, Dr. Ernesto Contreras, Sr., and since 1993, has overseen counseling at Oasis of Hope. His education includes a Master of Counseling, a Master of Business Administration, and a bachelor's degree in economics. In 1998, Kennedy founded the Worldwide Cancer Prayer Day after his father was healed of cancer. Along with oncologist Dr. Francisco Contreras, Kennedy is the co-author of *Fighting Cancer 20 Different Ways* and *Dismantling Cancer.*

In his personal mission to help others, Kennedy combines music and counseling and has participated in concerts and speaking engagements throughout the USA, Mexico, Japan, Kenya, Mexico, Spain, and The United Kingdom. His Spanish album, "Un Paso De Fe," is distributed by Latin American record label CanZion. www.danielkennedy.info   www.canzion.com

Foreword

When looking down the barrel of cancer, decisions are difficult to make because the stakes are at the highest. To find the balance between ignorance and information overload is a taxing challenge. The adversaries of fear and anxiety blockade the perception of hope. The intensity of emotions derails otherwise clear minds when the diagnosis is cancer. I know this from first hand experience.

On June 19th, 2007, I spent the night in the waiting room outside of the ER where doctors were trying to find out what was causing all of the pain my wife Carol was experiencing. By 2:00 AM, my wife urged me try to get some sleep. Wearily, I pulled some chairs together and attempted to get some sleep. The waiting room AC was on overdrive, thus the room was uncomfortably cold. I engineered a crude "cocoon" to keep warm. Laying across three chairs that were never designed to form a bed, I retracted my arms and head into my T-shirt, like a tortoise, hoping that my breath would warm me. Sometime between 3:00 AM and 4:00 AM, an Hispanic man – in his thirties – awakened me with the gentle words with a distinct Mexican accent, "Can I give you this blanket to keep you warm?" I sluggishly nodded, barely awakening. I have often wondered if this man was "for real," or if he was an angel. I do not know which he was. But he was a "sign," I believe, that some "warmth" would come from "across the border."

A few minutes after 6:00 AM, I got word from Carol that she would need to stay longer and that I should go home to get the kids off to school. I tiredly made the half hour freeway trek. Before I completed this mission with both children, the phone rang and my wife made an aphoristic request, "Come now." I told her that our son's bus passed by already but our daughter still needed to get to school. She responded firmly to come immediately.

I was shocked because she never responds that assertively. I asked what was wrong. She responded, "They found a mass." "A mass? What kind of mass?" I asked. She simply repeated, "A mass." I quietly stated, "I will come now."

This surely was not happening. My head was swirling as I drove the freeway – wondering what we really faced. The next few days were equally challenging to our emotional equilibrium. The news that it was cancer disoriented us and we had a hard time figuring out what to do. Our hours were filled with confusion and question marks.

On day two, or three, I found myself alone in the kitchen one night, having arrived at home from the hospital at midnight– out of groceries–with nothing to eat or drink. The lack of basic foods that night became a symbol of my despair. There I was trying to make decisions about how best to care for my wife, and I didn't even have groceries to provide a meal–something I hadn't had time for that day at the hospital. I was overwhelmed trying to manage life, let alone look through all of the cancer treatment options that are out there. I cried out, "God, I don't know how to win this battle. I need a strategy!"

I felt like I was going through a "knothole" clutching on to my wife's life trying to save it. But to get through, I couldn't clutch on to Carol's life. I needed to pray with arms and heart open to God. I resolved to tell God that no matter what the outcome would be, I would not fall to the advice of Job's wife to "curse God and die." Whether my wife would be alive six months later or not, I was resolved to love God. Slowly and painfully, we moved through the spiritual "knothole." Now I could begin to fight for her life in a new way – with an open palm rather than a clutched fist – with the blessing of God.

However, the chemotherapy did not go well. The nausea that predated the chemo continued to ravage her body.

In and out of the hospital she went. Standing at the foot of her bed one day, the doctor noted that he had Carol on seventeen different medications and he didn't know what else to do.

It was then that my administrative assistant found a book in my library that had been given to me earlier. It was written by Dr. Francisco Contreras and Daniel Kennedy. After a few phone calls and internet search, I sent a desperate midnight email to Mr. Kennedy saying, "I need help!" By the next morning a phone call came, with comforting words, "Get Carol down here now. We can help her."

I felt hope for the first time since the diagnosis. Even now, as I write this foreword, fully seventeen months after that initial communication, my eyes tear up when I recall that phone call.

When we were at the Contreras treatment center Oasis of Hope, I felt safe. I mean I felt really safe, as if I was in the palm of God's hand. Sharing Carol's hospital room – as is their "companion" program – I slept better than I had in months.

When we made our second trip down there, my mother-in-law, living in Texas, observed something simply from the tone of our voices when we would call her from Oasis of Hope Hospital, or from our home in San Diego. She correctly observed, "I know that you really value Oasis of Hope Hospital. You feel so much peace there. It seems to be such an important place for you." She was correct.

Carol went through much of the treatment that is outlined in this book and she is doing well now. In fact, the very day that I am writing this, we received another wonderful report regarding her cancer markers. I thank God with all of my heart.

We had the support of three oncologists in San Diego and after reviewing Carol's treatment plan and results from Oasis of Hope, one of our oncologists stated, "You are merging cancer protocols in a way that will help many others."

One day, after he had phoned us with the encouraging news of Carol's cancer markers, he exclaimed – knowing that we were following the Oasis of Hope protocol – "Whatever you are doing, keep doing it!"

At Oasis of Hope, we found an innovative approach to medicine. More importantly, we found hope. And most importantly, we experienced healing.

When you read this book, it will give you an idea of how we were supported. I trust that you will grow and begin to understand the potential that integrative cancer treatment has to help you. I believe the information contained within this book will be supremely helpful as it will bring a clarity of what can be done.

Before going to a new physician, we always pray, "Lord give us a doctor who is both competent and compassionate." Competency without compassion may be good for the body, but cold for the soul. Compassion without competency can mean that you are loved, but become more diseased. You will find that Dr. Contreras and Daniel Kennedy are both exceptionally competent and profoundly compassionate. And such are the rest of the team at Oasis of Hope.

Allow me to be deeply personal. Many years ago, a lady named Shary loaded her cancer ridden mother into the back of an old station wagon and drove from Arizona to the Oasis of Hope in Mexico. Shary, a woman of short stature, walked up behind Dr. Ernesto Contreras, Sr., a man with a marked height advantage.

Not knowing for certain who he was, she queried, "Are you Dr. Ernesto Contreras?" "I am" he replied, as he turned around. She looked up at him – their eyes meeting for the first time. Telling the story nearly four decades after the heavenly intersection occurred, through misty eyes, she now explains, "I discovered that I was looking into the eyes of Jesus!"

At the risk of being considered melodramatic, allow me to draw on this story. When I look into the eyes of Francisco Contreras – son of Ernesto, the Oasis of Hope founder – and when I look into the eyes of Daniel Ernesto Kennedy (Contreras) – grandson of Ernesto, the Oasis of Hope founder – I see the eyes of Jesus. I cannot possibly say more.

James L. Garlow, PhD
Senior Pastor, Skyline Church
San Diego, CA

Table of Content

Footprints

One night a man had a dream. He dreamed he was walking along the beach with the Lord. Across the sky flashed scenes from his life. For each scene he noticed two sets of footprints in the sand, one belonging to him, and the other to the Lord. When the last scene of his life flashed before him, he looked back at the footprints in the sand. He noticed that many times along the path of his life there was only one set of footprints. He also noticed that it happened at the very lowest and saddest times of his life. This really bothered him and he questioned the Lord about it. "Lord, you said that once I decided to follow you, you'd walk with me all the way. But I have noticed that during the most troublesome times in my life, there is only one set of footprints. I don't understand why, when I needed you most, you would leave me." The Lord replied, "My son, my precious child, I love you and I would never leave you. During your times of trial and suffering, when you see only one set of footprints, it was then that I carried you."

- Author Unknown

1

*The beginning of hope is the knowledge that
you do not walk the path alone.*

Your Healing Partner For Life

For a split second, the world stopped turning. War, famine, and disease all faded as our eyes fixated on America's hope for gymnastic gold…Nastia Liukin.[1] She only had to stick her dismount on the beam to secure Olympic gold in the women's all-around competition. She had competed with power, grace, and precision in the women's team competition at the 2008 Beijing Olympic Games. She excelled through the uneven bars, vault, balance beam, and floor routine. She set herself apart as a team leader and helped secure a silver medal for the women's team.

This was different. This was the women's individual all-around final. Twenty years earlier, in 1988, her father had missed his chance to secure all-around gold by one tenth of a point. At the 2005 World Championship, Nastia missed the all-around gold by one thousandth of a point. She needed to stick this dismount to build an insurmountable lead and secure the gold. She exploded off the beam tumbling powerfully through the air and planted both feet firmly in the mat. The medal was hers!

Nastia hardly achieved this historic moment alone. Her mother Anna, a former world champion gymnast, had been a role model for Nastia all of her life. Her father Valeri, who earned two gymnastic gold medals in 1988, had personally coached her since she was a toddler. And it wouldn't be fair not to mention her teammates and the team coordinator, Martha Karolyi, who cheered her on. No one attains greatness alone. Victory is built on the shoulders of dedicated team members that push the competitor to the heights of achievement.

The general public loves individual achievement, but when it comes to the Olympics, it is all about the medal count. The objective of the Olympic trials is to assemble a team of experts, functioning at the top of their game. We do this in order to increase the chances for all-around success. In 2008, the Olympic trials for gymnastics were held in Philadelphia. On June 22, Steve Penny, president of the United States Gymnastics Association, announced the names of the first two women to qualify for the squad in Beijing. Those two people were Nastia Liukin and Shawn Johnson. The selection process proved to be effective as both of these remarkable young athletes brought home a collection of Olympic medals, including one gold medal each.

Imagine what it must be like to posses the skills and talent to become an important and necessary piece of an amazing team. For most of us, the memories of the playground are far different. I remember lining up against the fence for kickball in elementary school and hoping that I would not be chosen last. Everyone wants to be a part of a team.

Once, I was selected by a group of coaches to play on the citywide championship basketball team. I admit that this hardly compared with going to the Olympics but I was thrilled just the same. I was a bit unsure why I had been chosen since I was fairly limited as an athlete. My individual contribution was minimal but my teammates made me better than I really was and I gained access to the winner's circle.

A Special Team

However, my understanding of the importance of "team" was radically altered in my first years working at the Oasis of Hope cancer treatment center. I will never forget the team captain. She was a precocious little 5-year-old who carefully assessed the situation and decided that she was going to recruit and assemble the team she needed. First, she enlisted her aunt to organize medications and doctor's appointments. Next, she placed her mother in charge of food preparation. Then, she entrusted her sister with the task of rubbing her back on sleepless nights. She continued to construct a team of "specialists" whose collective efforts she needed.

Then came the day when she drafted me onto the team. She decided that I would be the one to hold her anytime she was to receive an injection. So, each day when the time for treatment arrived, the phone in my office rang and I would drop everything and rush downstairs to do my part. I had never had a more challenging or important assignment. Her sweetness, tenacity, and charm are forever engraved in my soul.

This child understood the importance of a committed team of healing partners. From the heart and mind of this young girl came incredible wisdom. She inspired a commitment in me to be her healing partner for life. It is this concept of a committed team focused on a collective and life-long effort that has impacted how we strive to care for those who put their trust in the Oasis of Hope.

Over the last two decades, it has been my honor to partner with thousands of patients and their families, as they seek to restore quality of life and significantly increase their longevity. To be invited into a person's inner circle of confidence in spite of their physical, emotional, and spiritual vulnerability, is something I take very seriously. I believe that the patient-doctor relationship is sacred. I love the human spirit and I am inspired by the Holy Spirit to be a part of a patient's support system. I am not afraid to hope for each one of my patients.

It is my privilege to hope for those who cannot find the strength to hope for themselves. My resolve comes from the experience and profound example of the Oasis of Hope founder, my father, Dr. Ernesto Contreras, Sr.. He worked with patients who considered a cure to be the only acceptable outcome, and tenderly helped them to see that the number of days one lives is less important than how one lives each day. While many patients could only see the light at the end of the tunnel, I watched my father liberate patients from a mentality that limited what God could do along the way.

My dad was the first healing partner I ever met. He would sit down with his patients and say, "Look. I am your doctor. I will offer you non-harmful medicines that I would not hesitate to take myself. They will help you recuperate your health. However, I want you to understand that you are the team captain. You must actively participate in your healing. We will need to form a life-long partnership. Think of it like a business, only healing will be our objective and longevity will be our profit."

Dr. Contreras, Sr. realized that total health meant being well in body, mind, and spirit. In the early years, he invited a psychologist and a minister to work alongside him. In this way he could support every need of his patients. In 1963, he instituted a concept that involved the assembly of a multi-disciplinary team of expert healing partners. Dr. Ernesto Contreras, Sr. was a true visionary. The little girl I mentioned earlier in this chapter asked him to be on her team, as well. She simply called him "Tito," the Spanish word for Grandpa.

Support is Key

In general, when a person is diagnosed with cancer, the tendency is to become socially withdrawn. This is a counterproductive and antiquated response. I mean, this is what dinosaurs used to do when they got sick…they waltzed off to the tar pits. In fact, the thing to do is exactly the opposite. If one is to be victorious over cancer, a team of specialists must be put together to help the patient through the difficult times and push him or her up to the heights of healing success.

The Oasis of Hope has assembled a phenomenal team of specialists. We employ expert physicians, surgeons, and radiologists who contribute vital expertise. We have nurses with decades of experience caring for our patients. We have researchers with an impressive array of advanced degrees working on new therapies. We have applied nutritionists tapping the power of foods for our patients' benefit. We have physical therapists helping patients recuperate quickly. We have counselors bolstering the emotional strength of our patients. We have educators teaching patients how to make necessary lifestyle changes. We have prayer partners interceding for each patient. We have worked hard to assemble a team of experts committed to supporting a patient in every way that is needed to advance the healing process. Each member makes unique contributions to patient wellness. This is what we mean when we say that Oasis of Hope wants to be your healing partner for life.

Yet, having a competent, committed, and caring team of specialists is only the first step toward healing. This step must be complimented by an environment that draws all these resources together in a way that they can strategically intervene in a patient's life. Each patient needs a place of healing just as a desert wander needs an oasis.

Donald Factor

My vision for every patient that comes to Oasis of Hope is that he or she never loses *hope*, because the art of *medicine* is ever evolving means for *healing*. Donald Factor is a living testament to this philosophy…

- Dr. Contreras

"I was living ninety miles outside of London, in November of 1986, when I was diagnosed with carcinoma of the lung that had spread to my liver. The doctors in England didn't hold a lot of hope for me. They were very apologetic and offered a treatment which they thought might extend my life for a little while, but not for very long. I didn't feel like accepting that prognosis and decided to go and see Dr. Contreras. I'd met Dr. Contreras a few years before in a conference my wife and I had helped organize at Warwick University. I was very impressed with his approach. He told us he used modern medicine combined with natural therapies and a lot of love and faith. My wife Anna and I traveled from England to Los Angeles and then we drove down to the hospital where I was treated. When I arrived, I was in an extremely weak condition. It was ten days after the original diagnosis and the cancer had spread to my spine. I was in excruciating pain. My sciatic nerve had been affected so I could hardly walk. I was loosing weight rapidly too. They took a look at me at the Contreras clinic and were quite concerned. They were not very optimistic about my future either, but as Dr. Contreras Sr. said, because both my wife and I were very committed to doing everything possible to beat the cancer, they were prepared to work with us. To make a long story short, we succeeded.

I was very impressed with Dr. Contreras' clinic when I went inside and met the people. I had never experienced a hospital where the doctors would treat me as a human being instead of a bunch of symptoms or a disease walking through the door. There was a team of people there who were interested in me and they were involving me in the course my treatment would take. I was being asked, I was being informed, and suddenly I was part of the team that was treating me. I wasn't just an object that was being treated. That was tremendous.

I learned later from some of the doctors at the Oasis of Hope that I was more riddled with cancer than any case they had seen before. There were quite a few times during the treatment process when I felt like giving up, and the guilt I felt for even entertaining those thoughts often weighed heavily on me. However, part of the program involved the counsel of a psychologist, who helped me to accept those emotions as a normal part of the healing process. This did much to relieve my guilt and raise my spirits considerably. Dr. Contreras said that my positive and determined attitude along with Anna's enthusiasm helped me immeasurably.

After the initial treatment and about a year of home therapy, I was totally clear of any sign of cancer. Although I will probably never know if any one part of my experience was the actual key to my recovery, I am convinced that it was most likely all of it— everything, physical, emotional, and spiritual."

Donald Factor
England

2

*In the distance, the desert wanderer caught a glimpse
of a tomorrow.*

An Oasis of Hope

If you've ever spent a lazy afternoon channel surfing your local cable company's program menu you may have tuned in to one of those wilderness shows like "Man vs. Wild."[1] Shows like these are usually hosted by a rugged, ex-special forces type guy. At the start of the show, the host is kicked out of a moving Hummer, or dropped out of an airplane, or flung off of a boat, or fired from a cannon. He lands in a remote location where no sane human being would wish to find themselves.

The goal of the show is to teach viewers how to function when stranded in a wilderness location. The host is equipped with minimal supplies like a good knife, a water bottle, a flint stone, and a AAA card. The host narrates the experience for the viewer while navigating difficult terrain, constructing shelter against the elements, and foraging for food and fresh water.

It occurs to me that one of the reasons I get so engrossed in these shows is the parallels they present with my line of work. While I was certainly not kicked out of a moving Hummer or dropped out of an airplane, I find myself in difficult terrain each day as I help people to understand, avoid, and manage disease.

Bear Grylls is the host of the show "Man vs. Wild." He served three years as a survival instructor in the Special Air Service Regiment of the British Army and has close to twenty years of experience as an outdoor adventurer. I never feel nervous watching the episodes because it is clear that he knows exactly where to go and what to do.

I used to think how anxious and overwhelmed I would feel if I was stranded in some remote location. I wouldn't have the first clue in which direction to travel, how to make proper shelter, or where to find food. However, if someone like Bear Grylls were with me, it would be a great comfort to be able to place my trust in his knowledge and experience.

Wrap-around Care

In the same way, people managing a disease experience overwhelming anxiety because they know a difficult task lies ahead and they don't have the first clue how to get it done. Oasis of Hope is committed to relieving that anxiety. An important component of "wrap-around" care is the connection with an experienced medical team. The quality of that connection should serve to eliminate anxiety and develop confidence and trust.

I remember a story I heard at a convention once about a workaholic father who finally got around to taking his young son out fishing. They spent the rainy day on the lake casting lures into every imaginable nook and cranny of the shoreline. They caught nothing. Later, that night the father wrote in his diary, "Rained like crazy, caught nothing, worst day ever." Several days later he happened to see a picture his son had drawn at school spread out on the kitchen table. He picked it up. It was a drawing of the two of them fishing in the rain. Below the picture his son had written, "Dad and I went fishing. It rained all day and we didn't catch anything. Best day of my life."

I remember being struck by the truth of that story. Each and every experience in life is unique to the individual. The same is true in regard to illness. People experience illness differently. The body, mind, and spirit of a person react in ways that are unique to the individual. This is why the "one size fits all" approach to the treatment of disease has been such a huge failure.

There is no "one size fits all" set of treatments in the management of disease. Oasis of Hope understands that this is why it is critical for a medical team to develop a close relationship with each patient. The closer the connection with the patient, the easier it is to tailor a treatment program that is truly effective and that puts the patient at ease. True "wrap-around" care involves the support of a team that truly knows the patient as a unique individual.

Meeting The Needs & Relieving Stress

Needless to say, patients want to know that the doctors they have placed their trust in can positively impact the disease that ails them. Understandably, they want to feel better. The first step to feeling better is actually two-pronged. This step involves supplying the body with the fuel it needs and protecting the body from the stress factors that attack it.

Have you ever noticed how good food tastes when you're hungry? One time I took a long road trip to visit family. They were a good ten to twelve hours away and I got a late start. Because they lived in the mountains, I was concerned that if I didn't make good time I would have to drive up the hill after sundown and would be trapped in bad weather. So, I decided to drive straight through in order to beat the sun. I stopped only to get gas and use the restroom.

When I arrived, I was so famished I had begun to gnaw on the collar of my leather jacket to stave off the hunger pangs. They made me Campbell's tomato soup and served it with a handful of Saltines. If you've never had them before, Saltines are crackers that taste a bit like Styrofoam, only not as moist. Yet, that night, I was amazed at how good those crackers tasted!

When the body is ailing, it needs food desperately. However, the body has a set of specific needs in regard to food. The night of my arduous road trip I would have eaten anything.

If they had served me tree bark in a demi-glace of motor oil, I would have loved it! But an ailing body needs food that will optimize its ability to resist and control the development and progression of disease. Oasis of Hope recognizes that true "wrap-around" care includes the provision of a diet that bolsters the body's ability to do exactly this.

It is equally important, however, to shield the body from the elements in the day-to-day environment that depresses the body's ability to manage illness. Have you ever been subjected to extreme heat or cold before? Have you ever noticed how your body responds to those conditions?

Whenever I visit the northeast in the winter, I laugh in disbelief at the weather report in the morning. Some well-groomed guy will stand in front of the satellite picture and say, "Today we'll have a high of 5 below and a low of 20 below." A high of 5 below? Are you kidding me? It would be more accurate to say, "Today we'll have a low of 5 below and a really, really low of 20 below."

I shut down in those conditions. I don't care how many layers of clothing you put on me. You can bundle me up like Nanook of the North, but the first icy blast that knifes through those layers of clothing will send me right back to the hotel room. The same is true for extreme heat.

I've been to places so hot and humid that you actually sweat in the shower. Now that's ridiculous! Talk about an exercise in futility. That's the kind of weather where you put on shorts and a tank top and park yourself in front of the air conditioning vent.

Similarly, there are conditions that can arise at the cellular level that place tremendous stress on the body. Just like we tend to shut down in extreme conditions, these external stress factors compromise our body's ability to fend off illness effectively. We recognize that "wrap around" care also involves helping patients to eliminate these stress factors. This is an integral part of the physician-patient relationship at Oasis of Hope.

Caring For The Whole Person

But the body should never be the sole focal point of an effective treatment program. Emotional strength is a critical piece that has a huge impact on patient response to treatment. I remember talking with a friend once who had been an outstanding relief pitcher in college. He had played for the University of Arizona, a powerhouse in college baseball. His career was cut short by a back injury he sustained in a car accident.

I told him that I had been to a San Diego Padres game once and they had set up a pitching booth just inside the entry gate. This booth had a radar gun set up and would measure how fast you threw the ball. I gave it a whirl. Let me tell you, I threw that thing with all my might…several times. I barely broke 70 mph, a far cry from the high 90s that major league pitchers reach. No one else got even close either.

So, I told my friend that it seemed to me that the ability to throw the ball at those speeds must be exceedingly rare and that people who can stand a good chance of having a career in baseball. He told me I couldn't be more wrong. He said that there are lots of people who can throw a baseball in the high 90s with accuracy and that the vast majority of them will never set foot on a pitching mound because they don't have what it takes to be a pitcher.

I asked him what it took to be a successful pitcher, if it wasn't the ability to throw the ball at high speed accurately. He pointed to his head and said, "The vast majority lack the mental strength needed to pitch." He told me the mark of a professional pitcher is the ability to completely forget the last pitch thrown and focus only on the next pitch.

He said the greatest pitchers are unaffected by balls and strikes, hits and homeruns. They push everything out of mind and remain positive and focused on the present moment. They live in the "now."

In like manner, true "wrap-around" care helps patients to develop the emotional strength that allows them to really begin living in the "now." It is so important to teach people how to remain calm, positive, and action-oriented because these things have a huge impact on treatment success. We are determined to provide the kind of support that strengthens a patient's mental framework at Oasis of Hope.

Once, I witnessed a powerful object lesson involving a huge ball of kite string. The speaker stood in the front of the auditorium and asked for two volunteers. A couple of young men went up front and the speaker instructed one to grab the loose end of the string and walk back through the audience with it and continue right out the back door of the room.

When the young man was out of sight in the foyer the speaker yelled for him to stop. Then, he handed the ball of twine to the other volunteer and told him to walk through the curtain and backstage with it. When the second young man had stopped out of sight, the speaker took a black Sharpie marker from the podium and made a small dot on the white string. "This string stretching out to places we cannot see represents eternity," he said, "and this tiny dot represents the span of human history."

There was silence in the room for a minute. Finally, he said, "Our perspective is so tiny and limited, but God sees the whole stretch of eternity at once. Like eternity, God is bigger in every way than we can possibly imagine. The true scope of His power, love, and mercy absolutely defy human understanding." I was shaken a bit. There have been many studies regarding the impact of faith on a person's health, but it occurred to me that it is possible that the true measure of that impact defies human understanding.

Spiritual Fortitude

I am convinced that a firm grounding in Christ is essential for people managing disease. The powerful peace that stems from right relationship with God and man as outlined in Scripture cannot be found anywhere else. A deep-rooted knowledge of mercy, forgiveness, reconciliation, relationship, purpose, promise, heaven, and eternity grows a hope that strengthens a person's ability to remain calm, positive, and action-oriented through the most difficult of circumstances. It is the glue that holds us together. Oasis of Hope recognizes the importance of spiritual strength as a critical component to effective "wrap-around" care.

The name Oasis of Hope is not some catchy marketing ploy; it is who we are and how we operate as a treatment facility that embraces a body, mind, and spirit approach. There are two common definitions of the word "oasis." The first describes an oasis as "a small area in a desert that has a supply of water and is able to support vegetation." I like this definition because it does describe some of what a good treatment facility should provide.

Traveling across a desert is a stressful experience that pushes the body to its limits. This is why an oasis is such a welcome sight. It provides water and food to the traveler sorely in need of fuel. In addition, it provides shelter from the harsh surroundings. In the same way, the Oasis of Hope provides its patients with the medicinal and nutritional fuel they need to effectively manage disease, while sheltering them from the stress factors that weaken the immune system and contribute to the progression of disease.

However, the primary definition of oasis falls flat in one area. Travelers can't take a desert oasis with them. They can rest there temporarily but they must move out eventually and leave the support the oasis provides behind. For this reason, the Oasis of Hope is more like the secondary definition of the word oasis. This definition describes an oasis as "a situation offering relief in the midst of difficulty."

The strength of a true "wrap-around" care facility like Oasis of Hope is the understanding that disease management demands a life-long partnership between physician and patient. If doctors wish to make a long-lasting impact on a patient's body, mind, and spirit, they must commit to a permanent collaborative partnership. They must become "life coaches" and help patients make the kind of changes that will effect long-lasting healing.

The strength of Oasis of Hope is that the support structure that is tailor-made for a patient there is portable. It is 24 hour a day, 7 day a week, 365 day a year support designed to maximize the effectiveness of treatment and the quality of life for each and every patient. Nobody should have to manage an illness by themselves. This is not a road that is meant to be walked alone. Oasis of Hope is driven to walk that road with the patient…body, mind, and spirit.

May Kyle Orr

As it was once said, showing up is half the battle. The other half is your perseverance. One of the most important advantages of our therapy is the fact that it is permanent. It does not have to be stopped due to toxic or adverse effects. This permits a patient to be committed and perseverant, May Kyle Orr exemplifies this...

- Dr. Contreras

"My first visit to the Oasis of Hope Hospital was in January 2004, after being diagnosed with breast cancer in November 2003. I found out about the hospital through a person in my sister's church, who had only recently been in contact with someone who had visited the hospital. It came highly recommended and seemed to back up my belief in alternative treatments. After much research via the Internet and prayer, I realized that this was where I had to go.

My first visit lasted for 28 days during which I got ozone treatment and a mastectomy. This, however, did not result in a typical hospital experience — stuck indoors after each daily treatment. I was able to go for a walk along the beach or to the shops. The food on offer is a big part of the on-going treatment. It is based on a very strict diet. Also, on offer was nutritional classes that teach you the best way to make your food when you return home.

I am now at the end of my five year program, which has included 10 visits. Each visit, which was approximately every six months but only for a couple of days, has been very similar. This would include a check-up and consultation with the doctor, a blood test being taken for the tumor marker, and the opportunity to take home my prescribed medication due to the distance travelled, and only staying at the hospital for a few days. It gave me the opportunity to visit some lovely cities in the US before flying home.

I now plan to visit once per year so that the doctors can continue to physically monitor my progress. I am so, so glad that I made this decision instead of the conventional treatment (chemotherapy, radiation therapy) and side effects (hair loss, sickness, feeling tired, etc.), none of which I experienced but would have been my only option in the UK. I was also treated as an individual case, with treatments to suit my situation instead of as a general person, like back home, who generally always get the same treatments regardless."

May Kyle Orr
Scotland

3

*The final outcome of a system should be greater
than the sum of its parts.*

Integrative Regulatory Therapy

One of the really cool things about living in the age of technology is the host of "new" gadgets that crop up every few minutes. I exaggerate, of course, but it is common knowledge that when a technological product finally reaches the shelves for consumer purchase it is already obsolete.

Take the tabletop computer Microsoft is developing called "Milan," for example.[1] The concept is simple. What if your tabletop could turn on and you could use your fingers to do all the things that a mouse cursor can do? What if you could select a program, pull down menus, operate scroll bars, move and resize objects, all with the tips of your fingers. Pretty cool, huh? I always love it when I see something new and exciting coming down the road. New things open up exciting avenues of change.

I've got news for you. In the world of cancer treatment it is time for something innovative. For too many years, we have labored in vain to find a cure for the disease. A new approach is here and it brings with it exciting avenues of change in regard to cancer treatment. I want to offer those with cancer a hope for a better tomorrow.

The quest for the cure for cancer is admirable if not noble. Over the last four decades, researchers have made monumental efforts to thoroughly examine and understand cancer. Investigators have worked hard to learn all they can about the causes of cancer, the nature of cancer, and the principles that govern the growth and spread of cancer. They have examined the primary tumors found in breast cancer, colon cancer, lung cancer, prostate cancer, and others.

In the laboratories of academia and industry, researchers have attacked cancer cells with every imaginable tool and substance. In the halls of medicine, clinicians have used hundreds of advanced surgical procedures to remove tumors, a variety of methods to burn malignancies, and an arsenal of chemotherapeutic agents to destroy cancer in the most hidden corners of the body.

In over thirty-five years, the medical community has spent hundreds of billions of dollars researching new cancer treatments but failed to significantly impact the incidence of cancer or the cancer mortality rate. Why is it that the world's greatest minds blessed with virtually unlimited funding have struggled to make even the humblest dent in the cancer epidemic? One significant factor is that cancers can mutate and become resistant to chemotherapy and radiation. This is especially true once cancer spreads.

A patient's chances of survival are much higher when the cancer is caught early and the tumor is still localized, because then it can be totally removed. Yet, by stage IV the cancer has spread, or metastasized, to other organs. This is where things get extremely complicated and the treatment options become exceedingly dangerous. Unfortunately, many patients don't find out that they have cancer until it has reached stage IV. This is because early stage cancer doesn't necessarily present a host of tell-tale symptoms. Often, the first recognizable symptoms appear when it has already spread to other locations. Imagine feeling fine one day and the next day receiving a somber diagnosis from your doctor. The effect is devastating.

Too many people find out they have cancer when an oncologist looks them in the eye and tells them that it is already "too late." This is where the search begins for a treatment option that can treat the "untreatable." Many patients and families become torn between conventional and alternative medicine. Let me explain some of the differences between the two.

Conventional Vs. Alternative

In conventional medicine, the focus is the disease. In alternative medicine, the focus is the patient. Let's discuss conventional cancer treatment first. The goal of conventional oncology therapies—chemotherapy, radiation, and surgery—is tumor eradication. Each of these three interventions can be extremely effective when used properly. In many cases, any one of the treatments will be the most appropriate to indicate for a patient and should be used.

An ethical oncologist must recognize the many short comings and failings of conventional therapy, however. Most everyone is aware of the negative side effects of chemotherapy, radiation, and surgery. They are immuno-depressant and kill healthy cells as well as malignant cells. This can take a terrible toll on the patient's quality of life and in some cases will actually shorten the patient's life. But, there is an issue much more significant than the drawbacks of the side effects. Cancer cells become resistant to therapy over time. Unfortunately, many patients that experienced a good outcome at first with chemotherapy or radiation will find that they no longer respond as well on subsequent cycles. Conventional medicine can be part of the solution but it is limited and rarely extends the life of stage IV cancer patients for very long. This is why thousands of people seek out alternatives. Considering that less than 20% of people with stage IV breast cancer will survive longer than one year, it is understandable that many people want to see if there is another more promising approach.

The term "alternative medicine" can mean just about anything under the sun from vegan diets and juice regimens to reflexology and magnet therapy. The main focus and belief of alternative cancer treatment is that the immune system of the patient must be boosted back in a healthy balance. Then, the body will heal itself of any illness from heart disease to diabetes to cancer. Juicing, vitamin and mineral supplements, detoxification, and immune system building all have great merit. The truth is that God designed the human body with great abilities to heal itself. The body even has immune system cells that are specifically tasked with killing mutated cells. But, alternative medicine has many deficiencies as well.

To start, just as there are many oncologists that know nothing about nutrition, there are many alternative medicine clinics that don't have oncologists on staff, that is to say that there is nobody that was formally trained in cancer treatment. There is also often a great lack of clinical trials that support the use of many alternative interventions. But here is the biggest shortcoming of alternative cancer treatments. Many cancers are just too aggressive to respond to purely natural medicine.

For years, oncologists have criticized alternative medicine doctors and accused many of being scam artists. Alternative doctors fought back stating that the failure rates of chemotherapy are unacceptable and that the treatments make the patients suffer more than the disease. The great news is that there is an emerging trend in cancer treatment called "Integrative Medicine." This approach combines conventional medicine with alternative interventions that help overcome and compensate for the deficiencies of chemotherapy, radiation, and surgery. The traditional medicine is still used for tumors that are too aggressive to be treated by alternative medicine alone. The alternative interventions, however, help maintain the tumors treatable. Through alternatives, patients can tolerate the treatment and the negative side effects can be diminished, and the immune system can be preserved.

Oasis of Hope is the trendsetter with more than 45 years of experience in integrative cancer treatment. It is followed by Cancer Treatment Centers of America with over 25 years of experience and now major centers such as Sloan-Kettering, MD Anderson and others are starting to enhance their therapies using complimentary medicine. The National Cancer Institute now has a department of complimentary medicine. This is all great news for cancer patients around the world. Hopefully these major centers will graduate from complimentary medicine up to the major leagues of integrative medicine! Oasis of Hope continues to be in a class of its own however, because our approach is not just about what treatments we use; it is more about the whole treatment experience that we provide our patients. It is a beautiful blend of medical competence and caring, of art and science, of faith, hope and love.

There is Hope

Close to 90% of the patients that come to the Oasis of Hope arrive with late stage cancers. Often, they feel hopeless because they have been told that there is nothing more that can be done and that they should go home and get their affairs in order. Nothing could be further from the truth. There is always hope.

However, as long as people cling to the idea that the only hope for a cancer patient is the complete elimination of the tumors and that chemotherapy is the only treatment that can achieve this goal, few people will be able to "overcome" cancer. Aggressive treatment is often prescribed but it comes at a high price. Patients must suffer serious loss in regard to quality of life. Most people experience unpleasant to unbearable side effects. Statistics tell us that, more often than not, chemotherapy will fail to destroy the tumors completely because cancer naturally develops resistance to treatment. Malignant cells have a way of figuring out how to protect themselves so that they become increasingly more difficult to kill over time. Positive results are often short-lived and when the tumor stops responding to one treatment, oncologists turn to increasingly aggressive treatments until the cancer becomes untreatable.

If you find yourself in these circumstances, please allow me to speak directly to you for a moment. To begin with, you are not a statistic. You are a person living with cancer and there are some options available to you that you may not have heard of yet. Your natural strengths can help you respond to this threat. Please do not discount the possibility of a miracle in your life.

The other thing I want you to know is the field of molecular biology has made a number of significant breakthroughs, helping scientists and doctors understand the nuts and bolts of malignant cells and their behavior. In addition, the medical community has developed less aggressive chemotherapies and found effective ways to minimize side effects. For more than two decades I was an outspoken opponent of chemotherapy, but that was only because the treatment made patients suffer and rarely prolonged their lives for a significant amount of time. Chemotherapy by itself is still of little value. However, chemotherapy that is used as one element in an integrative medicine regimen can be extremely effective. Now that is exciting news!

In the past, I refused to prescribe chemotherapy because I would never prescribe it to myself. How then, could I justify administering the treatment to my patients? However, new research has helped our clinical research team understand that the shortcomings of chemotherapy can be overcome. Chemotherapy is not effective as a stand-alone treatment, but when used as a small part of a comprehensive treatment approach, it becomes a powerful anti-cancer weapon.

A New Approach To Cancer Control

Integrative Regulatory Therapy, or IRT, is the integration of therapies that have a powerful synergistic effect upon each other. Synergy is what happens when forces work together so that the total effect is greater than the sum of the forces. Chemotherapy, or cytotoxic therapy, is just one element of the Oasis of Hope treatment approach which our scientists have registered as Integrative Regulatory Therapy. The other seven elements are every bit as important and compelling. Let me begin to share with you what the Oasis of Hope difference is by giving you an overview of IRT and then I will break each of the treatment components down for you in the subsequent chapters.

IRT is designed to destroy cancer cells, delay their growth and mutagenesis, and impede their spread for as long as possible. It is also designed to maximize the amount of time a patient enjoys a high quality of life. Let's look at each component briefly.

Oxidative Preconditioning

The first component of IRT is Oxidative Preconditioning Therapy. When the cells of our bodies are exposed to large quantities of oxidants, a condition called oxidative stress occurs and often results in tremendous damage. The body produces a number of natural antioxidants to try and prevent oxidative stress from occurring. Cytotoxic chemotherapy often creates hazardous levels of oxidative stress, not only in the cancer, but also in the body's healthy normal tissues.

Oxidative Preconditioning Therapy is intended to boost the capacity of the body's normal tissues to withstand the oxidative stress imposed by cytotoxic chemotherapy. Exposing cells to an acute and repeated mild oxidant stress, such as the one produced by ozone autohemotherapy, increases the antioxidant defense system. In ozone autohemotherapy, about 200 ml of a patient's blood are withdrawn, and this blood is exposed to ozone and UV light. This treated blood is then reinfused into the patient. The reinfused blood contains oxidized compounds, which serve as a signal of oxidative stress to the body's normal healthy tissues, reflexively causing them to increase their production of protective antioxidant enzymes. Repeated sessions of ozone and UV autohemotherapy prior to chemotherapy insure that the body's normal tissues are in much better condition to cope with the oxidative stress imposed by the subsequent chemotherapy. Thus, the intent of Oxidative Preconditioning Therapy is to make therapy more tolerable for the patient while simultaneously improving the ability of the therapy to destroy the tumor!

Cytotoxic Therapy

The second component of IRT is Cytotoxic Therapy, which is designed to destroy cancer cells directly by poisoning them. Because we couple Cytotoxic Therapy with Oxidative Preconditioning Therapy, the cancer-killing effects of cytotoxic therapy are maximized while the negative side effects from it are reduced significantly. Our cytotoxic therapies include a range of well-known chemotherapeutic drugs.

Cell Signal Transduction Therapy

The third component of IRT is Cell Signal Transduction Therapy, which, by using nutraceuticals (vitamin supplements with medicinal qualities manufactured at a pharmaceutical grade) and safe drugs to target "cell signaling pathways" in cancer cells, will make cancer cells easier to kill, while suppressing their capacity to grow, spread to distant organs, and evoke the growth of new blood vessels that feed tumors. "Signal transduction" refers to the way in which cellular proteins undergo small, and usually reversible changes, in their structure to induce alterations in cell behavior. The genetic material of cancer cells is typically altered in ways that over-activate intracellular signaling pathways that promote unregulated growth and spread of cancer cells; or that make them harder to kill with chemotherapy or radiotherapy. Cell Signal Transduction Therapy seeks to inhibit these overactive signaling pathways, making cancers easier to kill and control.

Redox Regulatory Therapy

The fourth component of IRT is Redox Regulatory Therapy, which selectively targets tumor sites with intense levels of oxidative stress. This means that the therapy is designed to attack tumor cells only and present no harm to healthy tissue. The combination of high-dose intravenous vitamin C therapy, coupled with ozone autohemotherapy and the oxygen-carrier Perftec, achieves this desirable effect. The result is a therapy that can effectively hold tumor growth at bay while boosting the killing effect of concurrent cytotoxic therapy.

Immune Stimulation Therapy

The fifth component of IRT is Immune Stimulation Therapy, designed to aid the immune system's ability to attack cancer by optimizing the function of natural killer cells and cytotoxic T-cells. The therapy employs a two-pronged approach. The first prong involves the use of natural products that boost the function of the immune system. The second prong involves the use of substances that block the mechanisms tumors use to suppress the immune system.

Diet & Exercise

The sixth component of IRT is significant improvement in regard to diet and exercise. The evidence from the world around us of the preventative and curative benefits of a diet low in fats and animal proteins is compelling. In addition, the preventative and curative benefits of regular aerobic exercise have been widely acknowledged by the medical community for decades. More recent research suggests that these healthful lifestyle strategies may also help to slow the growth and spread of many pre-existing cancers. So prudent advice on diet and lifestyle is a key component of therapy at Oasis of Hope.

Emotional Support

The seventh component of IRT is the development of an emotional support structure, not only in hospital but at home, as well. The management of cancer can tax the strongest individual; the energy required to learn about the illness, embrace treatment, and alter lifestyle creates a need for an external emotional support system that serves to strengthen and refresh the patient. We seek to provide that support structure principally because it has a powerful impact on the entire IRT program.

Spiritual Support

The eighth component of IRT is the development of spiritual security. There is no question that the fear and anxiety produced by the possibility of death coupled by an insecurity regarding the afterlife can have a significant impact on a patient's overall physical and emotional state. Therefore, we seek to provide avenues for patients to develop the hope, peace, and security that stems from a healthy relationship with God. This, too, will positively impact a patient's ability to engage in the whole process of disease management.

Well-trained oncologists do not "fly blind" when it comes to selecting therapies for a patient. They make educated and accurate decisions regarding the strategies that are likely to be useful with a given type of cancer. However, because every cancer is truly unique, there is never certainty that a given therapy will be effective and, because cancers are constantly evolving, even a therapy that was highly effective once may prove less effective when used again. IRT can adapt to these changes. This is why we hope that the IRT offered at Oasis of Hope becomes the trend within the medical community.

Abraham Lincoln said, "You can fool some of the people all of the time, and all of the people some of the time, but you cannot fool all of the people all of the time." The same can be said for cancer cells. These cells may be able to avoid some therapies all of the time, and all of the therapies some of the time, but they cannot avoid all of the therapies all of the time. When doctors address a cancer from multiple focal points simultaneously, with treatments which have a synergistic effect on each other, the cancer cannot avoid everything.

These are the concepts behind Oasis of Hope's Integrative Regulatory Therapy. We embrace the knowledge gained from close to four decades of research. We accept the honest assessment that it is highly unlikely a "wonder cure" is about to appear from some pharmaceutical laboratory. We believe we must intervene simultaneously in as many ways as feasible to promote the death of cancer cells and halt the spread of tumors. Our Integrative Regulatory Therapy represents a credible, innovative strategy to achieve this. It is the hope, medicine, and healing that we seek to provide.

Burga Theresia Ratti

While you can judge an institution by their results, its real value lies on permanency. Nothing like longevity gives one reassurance and confidence in an institution. Our institution has survived relentless adversity and has exceeded all expectations of many critics and friends. Except for my mother, now 88, and myself, I was 11 years old when my father founded the Oasis of Hope and worked with my mom and dad in all areas of the hospital since then, after school and in the summers, no one else has traveled the whole stretch. Though there are some faithful and wonderful coworkers that have been with us 30+ years, what has blessed us more than anything are the miracles of life represented by patients that defied all odds and are still with us in spite of gloomy diagnosis. Burga is one, rather two, of those miracles. Here is her amazing story…

- Dr. Contreras

"I am very happy and grateful to be at Oasis of Hope. It is a very special place for me and I'm also happy to share my story with you. It was in summer of 1987, when my daughter just turned 11-years-old. At that time I went to the doctor and my second pregnancy was confirmed, so of course I was all very happy. At the same time, however there was a suspicion of breast cancer, which was confirmed two days later. So the doctor basically told me, in order to save my own life, I would have to follow the therapeutic plan which would be 1) To have a therapeutic abortion; 2) Have a mastectomy; 3) To have radiation; and 4) To have chemotherapy. All this one month after the diagnosis. I prayed to the Holy Spirit that night and the next morning, I knew I was going to keep the baby. We lived in Colorado at that time. We went down to the University Hospital and we told the doctor, 'We're keeping the baby.'

After we had made the decision to keep the baby, the rest of my pregnancy was really happy. At that time, I called Dr. Contreras, Sr.. I had heard his lecture in a health conference in Arizona in 1984. I said to myself that if we ever needed anybody to help us in the field of cancer, seeing him would make sense. His approach made sense. He was a beautiful warm person. I called him when I was pregnant and I told him what we had decided. We told Dr. Contreras, Sr. that we were going to keep the baby and asked him what he suggested. He said everything was okay and asked us to come down to the hospital after the baby was a few months old. Now my baby is 20-years-old. I think God is with me. However, the cancer did come back. When my new son was 5-months-old, we flew from Colorado down to the Oasis of Hope. We have been coming back to the hospital for so many years. I was doing pretty well for a while; I had some cancer setbacks.

In autumn 1991, we moved back to Europe. I was raised in Germany. Since we moved back, I have been coming back to the Oasis of Hope. All the spiritual support that I am getting here I am taking with me in my mind and in my thoughts. It has been 20 years since I have been coming to Oasis of Hope. The emotional support is great. We have sing-a-longs in the mornings; then again I don't know what the best part about being here is. I have cancer in the bones on my back and in my collar bone but it has been stable since 2000 and of course I am very grateful for that and this place. If you have cancer or any of your loved ones have cancer, check it out. Use the Internet or call. This is a holistic place, they just don't treat the body; they treat the person. Everybody is in the same great spirit here and it's a great place to be."

Burga Theresia Ratti
Bensheim, Germany

4

Weathering the storm depends on the preparations made before it hits.

People Get Ready

It was Louis Pasteur who said, "Chance favors the prepared mind," a profound statement that borders on the philosophical.[1] Pasteur would have agreed that each day is a seemingly endless stream of opportunities that fly past us. Yet, some people feel opportunity comes along very rarely. Why is there such a huge difference in perspective? The answer is simple.

Oxidative
Preconditioning

We can only take advantage of the opportunities we are prepared to see. Often, our preparedness depends on knowledge and training. For example, Sir Alexander Fleming was very well-educated. He was a bacteriologist, biologist, immunologist, and pharmacologist. Therefore, he was able to "see" an opportunity where others would have simply seen mold gathering in a Petri dish. It turned out that the mold (penicillium notatum) produced a chemical that killed bacteria he was culturing and...voila!... the first antibiotic was developed in 1929. Years of study had prepared Fleming to see an opportunity for discovery that others would have missed, or dismissed.

Preparation is a critical component in just about every walk of life. For example, farmers prepare the soil in order to ensure that their land will yield a good harvest. They till the soil to break down leftover crop residue and kill the weeds that can crowd out the future crop. They also take a variety of measures to prepare to counteract erosion from water and wind. Preparatory measures like windbreaks, cover crops, and contour farming all help the farmer get the most out of the land.

Athletes condition their bodies to compete. A friend who was a state champion wrestler shared with me that he used to do 800 push-ups and 800 crunches a day during the wrestling season. That way, his body was prepared to endure the physical stress of a top-level wrestling match.

So, I wonder. If preparation is a necessary factor that can determine success, shouldn't doctors prepare their patients for therapy? While one cannot guarantee an outcome, the chances of success increase exponentially when an opportunity is preceded by preparation. For patients living with life-threatening disease, a therapy represents an opportunity for healing. The more prepared a patient is, the higher the probability they will derive benefit from a therapy.

Surprisingly, careful patient preparation is a revolutionary concept in the world of cancer treatment. However, if you think about it, the idea is completely logical and the inability to embrace this logic is a major reason for the failed attempts to solve the cancer puzzle.

Oasis of Hope has been preparing the body, mind, and spirit of each patient for 45 years in an effort to increase the likelihood that a patient will experience success in the effort to halt the progression of disease and to increase overall quality of life.

Be Prepared

In this chapter, I want to focus on an extremely important type of physical preparation. Cytotoxic chemotherapies present a significant physical challenge to the body – in large part because they expose the body's healthy tissues to severe oxidative stress.

It is imperative that patients be pre-conditioned to withstand the physical challenge these therapies pose. Careful oxidative pre-conditioning can induce a state of tolerance to oxidative stress in healthy tissues that can dramatically reduce the side effects associated with chemotherapy.

I'm not a big fan of mixed martial arts competitions, but I did catch a very interesting show that featured an unusual training regimen practiced by UFC fighter Wanderlei Silva. [2] I was flipping through the channels and I caught a glimpse of this man with his nose taped shut and a snorkel strapped to his head. I put down the remote, fascinated.

This athlete was hurtling through one of the most grueling circuit training courses I have ever seen. For ten minutes, wearing a 40-pound vest, he ran up stairs and down stairs, executed jiu-jitsu maneuvers, jumped rope, lifted weights, performed push-ups, and breathed through a snorkel the entire time. Then he rested for forty seconds while his trainer took a blood sample from his finger before starting the circuit all over again. "What in the world is he doing?" I thought.

Then the fighter's trainer was interviewed. He explained that Wanderlei is a brawler, not a boxer. Because of this, he knew that his fighter was going to get hit often and early. When this happens the nasal cavity tends to bleed and breathing is restricted. The more difficult it is to get oxygen the faster muscles will tire.

So, he explained that the taped nose and snorkel create a hypoxic, or oxygen poor, environment for the fighter. They closely monitor the level of lactic acid in Wanderlei's blood between each circuit. The higher the levels of lactic acid, the more difficult it will be for Wanderlei to complete the circuit. The trainer explained that the hypoxic circuit training, as he called it, simulates the later rounds of a fight when breathing is restricted and muscles are fatigued. If the fighter can prepare for a fight in this environment, he will be able to withstand the stress of those conditions better when he encounters them in the ring.

47

Increasing Effectiveness Through Pre-Conditioning

In a way, this is a lot like oxidative pre-conditioning. We can prepare a patient to more effectively tolerate oxidative stress through an improved antioxidant response. And we can boost the expression of protective antioxidant enzymes in the body's healthy tissues by exposing the body to ozone-treated blood, in a procedure known as "ozone autohemotherapy" (O3-AHT).[3, 4]

The infusion of ozone into rats or humans induces oxidative stress in the body's tissues. These tissues respond by increasing their antioxidant defenses.[5-11] This is well documented in many studies – and in fact is almost commonsensical; it would be surprising if the body's tissues didn't respond to a mild oxidative stress by increasing their defenses. However, ozone infusion can be a bit risky – air embolism is a potentially devastating complication - which is why medical scientists have devised an alternative, safer way to achieve the same protective benefit. In O3-AHT, about 200 milliliters of a patient's blood are withdrawn; this blood is then blended with ozonated oxygen outside the body. This ozone rapidly reacts with cells and blood proteins in the drawn blood. Ozone is so unstable and reacts so rapidly that within seconds there is no ozone per se in the blood. However, there are many chemical compounds in the blood formed by reaction with the ozone that are similar to those produced in the body's tissues during oxidative stress.[12] The ozone-treated blood is then infused back into the patient. The patient's healthy tissues perceive these newly-formed chemical compounds as a sign of oxidative stress – and respond by boosting their antioxidant defenses.[11] In this way, antioxidant defenses can be boosted without directly exposing the body's tissues to oxidative stress. That's why O3-AHT is such a safe and well tolerated procedure. For over 50 years, this therapy has been used safely in millions of patients, primarily in Europe.

Virtually Side-effect Free

In 1980, a study done by the German Medical Society on ozone therapy polled 644 therapists who treated 384,775 patients and administered 5,579,238 ozone treatments. The study noted only 40 cases of side effects, representing a rate of .000007%. This number may not seem significant to the layman, but it establishes ozone as the safest medical therapy ever devised.

At Oasis of Hope, we use multiple sessions of O3-AHT to optimize the body's antioxidant defenses prior to administration of cytotoxic chemotherapies. We amplify the efficacy of the procedure by also exposing the ozonated blood to UV light, which, like ozone, induces oxidative stress in the withdrawn blood. In this way, the body's healthy tissues achieve a state of tolerance to the oxidative stress imposed by chemotherapy. Chemotherapy administered under these conditions is safer, and its side effects are less distressing to the patient.

O3-AHT has an additional benefit that makes it especially appropriate as an adjuvant for chemotherapy – it boosts blood flow to the tumor and aids oxygen delivery to parts of the tumor that are hypoxic (low in oxygen).[13] Many chemotherapies – and also radiotherapy – are less effective at killing cancer cells when oxygen levels are low. So O3-AHT, while protecting healthy tissues, may make cancer cells more vulnerable to chemotherapeutic assault. That's a good trick, isn't it! We will discuss the impact of ozone autohemotherapy on tumor oxygen delivery further where we discuss the effective use of vitamin C therapy.

So, why is it likely that you and your doctor have not heard about O3-AHT? The gears of change turn slowly in the U.S. medical community. In Europe, ozone therapy has been in use for 50 years by over 10,000 physicians, but in America ozone therapy is only taught privately, usually in naturopathic schools, so your family doctor is probably untrained in its use.

I would like to suggest that the Journal of the American Medical Association (JAMA) and the New York based World Health Organization (WHO) research the benefits of ozone usage in medicine. There are over 3,000 medical references in international peer reviewed medical journals showing the effectiveness and safety of ozone therapy for humans drawn from the studies of millions of dosages given over 50 years of clinical application.

Most of these reports have been published since 1990 and are easily accessible on Medline. They include pre-clinical studies, animal experiments, patient case histories, placebo-controlled double blind human trials, and clinical reviews. The authors come from Italy, Poland, Russia, Germany, Cuba, Spain, Israel, Japan, and America. The International Ozone Association and the manufacturer of the ozone generator report that over 7,000 doctors in Europe have used medical ozone safely and effectively, some for over 40 years. It is used less in the U.S. due to a misconception.

The caution is due to ozone's well-known toxicity. In the stratosphere, ozone acts as a shield, deflecting harmful UV rays. However, in the troposphere, ozone is a major component of smog. When we breathe it, ozone can cause serious pulmonary damage. Molecular oxygen (O_2) is a very stable gas, but ozone (O_3) is a very unstable oxygen gas because it possesses three oxygen molecules. The additional oxygen molecule makes ozone a highly reactive oxidant.

But the key fact to remember is that, during O3-AHT, the body's tissues are not exposed to ozone – but rather only to chemical compounds induced in blood by transient ozone exposure. That's why it is so safe.

Professor Richard A. Lerner, MD, is the Lita Annenberg Hazen Professor of Immunochemistry and holds the Cecil H. and Ida M. Green Chair in Chemistry at The Scripps Research Institute in La Jolla, California. Lerner worked with Associate Professor Paul Wentworth, Jr. PhD and a team of investigators and reported that antibodies can destroy bacteria through the production of the reactive gas ozone. In 2002, their article titled "Evidence for Antibody-Catalyzed Ozone Formation in Bacterial Killing and Inflammation" was published in the prestigious journal *Science*.[14]

"Ozone has never been considered a part of biology before," says Lerner. However, he goes on to explain that ozone may be part of a previously unrecognized killing mechanism that enhances the defensive role of antibodies by allowing them to subject pathogens to hydrogen peroxide. This may allow the antibodies to participate directly in the killing of pathogens. Furthermore, this research opens up exciting possibilities for new antibody-mediated therapies for conditions ranging from bacterial and viral infection to cancer.

If ozone is indeed produced naturally by the human immune system, even skeptics have conceded this would be of great significance and give merit to the concept of ozone as a medicine. Hopefully, more researchers like Dr. Lerner and Dr. Wentworth will encourage the pursuit of further research in the USA and around the world.

I am convinced that for every ounce of preparation spent, a pound is gained in tolerance and response to therapy. My goal is to share this information with oncologists worldwide because, without question, O3-AHT should rapidly become an essential tool in comprehensive treatment programs everywhere.

Carol Garlow

Carol Garlow is a perfect example of the enormous benefits of oxidative preconditioning. The advanced stage of her malignancy and its aggressiveness required highly potent chemo; but her precarious health status raised many red flags. Due to the protective effects of our IRT, in general, and oxidative preconditioning, in particular, she was able to endure the necessary treatments. This provided a big payoff. Here is her testimony...

- Dr. Contreras

"'Cancer! No, not me. Cancer is not even in my vocabulary.' That's what I was thinking when the doctor had walked into my cubicle in the emergency room at approximately 6:30 AM on June 20, 2007 and told me the CAT scan revealed a mass. The doctor sat on a small stool beside me, looking into my eyes and using words and phrases like 'omentum' 'peritoneum' and an 'ovarian cancer like mass.' I really could not fully comprehend the implications of those terms.

The first few days I was in shock and denial. The actual diagnosis was primary peritoneal carcinoma. I had prayed for healing for people who had cancer, but I had never dealt with it for myself. Emotions were raging inside of me.

I felt frustration that I had lost control of my life. I experienced anger, anxiety, and sadness – not merely for me – but for my family as I watched them deal with this diagnosis. It seemed to consume us. I eventually came to the point where I had to honestly face the cancer and my future. I had to accept the challenges ahead, and I did.

A major turning point for me was when I heard God's voice saying, 'Carol, you are going to have go through everything – but, I am going to be with you through it all.' As a result, I felt a peace and a resolve. God said He would be with me; my trust was in Him. Truly in Him. There I found strength that I could go through this dramatic experience, no matter what. I knew it would not be easy. Yet with the word I received from God, I had a resolve to move forward.

Psalm 27 – especially verses 4 and 5 – were very meaningful to me during the difficult days of recovery from surgery and then chemotherapy. These verses speak about the one desire of one's heart, which is to seek after Him. When you do, you will live in the house of the Lord. In times of trouble, you are safe, because God hides you in 'the secret place of His tabernacle.' After truly facing cancer head on, I knew I was in that secret place, safe and secure with God taking care of me.

A later verse (13), states, 'I would have lost heart, unless I had believed that I would see the goodness of the Lord in the land of the living.' I have a strong belief in God. However, in the natural I think I would have lost heart if I had not gone to Oasis of Hope. I was struggling with nausea and weakness, concerned whether I had enough strength to make it through.

Going to Oasis gave me hope that I could strengthen my immune system while killing any cancer cells that were still trying to consume me. I felt safe and secure there, even though I was not always feeling well.

Additional support came from my husband who stood beside me in many difficult moments. He spent many hours learning about cancer and the Oasis of Hope treatment protocol.

I knew I could trust him. Because of his steady encouragement to pursue the treatments at Oasis of Hope, I had confidence in the doctors' and the staff's knowledge of this disease. I trusted them and knew that they were speaking truth. I felt their personal concern for me, and their desire to take care of me as long as it would take.

To my husband, I want to thank you for your tireless support, love and care of me in this journey.

To Dr. Francisco Contreras, Daniel Kennedy, I say a deep heart felt thank you.

To all of the doctors and staff and to the "cocina" (kitchen) staff, I say thank you for all you have done and are still doing to preserve my life.

Not only have you helped me, but also the thousands of others who are likewise fighting for a quality of health and life. Thank you and many blessings to your endeavors of cancer research at Oasis of Hope Hospital. In the future, thousands more will need your love, compassion and hope you offer."

Carol Garlow
San Diego, CA
USA

5

Promoting longevity, energy, wellbeing...this is success.

The Case for Chemotherapy

This chapter is crucial for you. It exposes cancer, its threats, and also its weaknesses. It's crucial for me. It exhibits my view on cancer therapies, their potential, and their weaknesses. It's crucial for us, you, and me. It proposes opportunities and hope.

I remember the first time I read the science fiction novel *Fahrenheit 451* by Ray Bradbury.[1] Published in 1953, the book tells the story of firefighter Guy Montag, who begins to seriously question the values of the world around him.

At one point in the story, Montag desperately tries to communicate with his wife but she is entranced by the television screen that spans three of the four walls in their "viewing parlor" and she is unable to listen to him because of the earbud piping loud music and talk radio into her head.

It was clear as I progressed through the novel that the author, living in a time when only 1 in 10 households owned a television, and long before the invention of the iPod and Blue Tooth devices, recognized the importance of human interaction and saw coming technology as a threat to that interaction. I remember putting down that book and thinking about how much the American living room has changed.

In 1953, most living rooms had two couches, or seating arrangements, that faced each other. Sometimes, there was a low table in the middle. The layout might differ slightly from household to household, but there is no question that the living room of the 1950s was designed to facilitate human interaction.

The modern day living room is quite different. There is usually a large television prominently displayed against a featured wall. The furniture in the room is now arranged to face the television. Again, the layout will be slightly different from home to home, but the message is clear. The modern living room is for watching TV.

I remember realizing that this was an important concept to digest. Human interaction is important. There is no substitute for it. I remember realizing how easy it is to let things encroach upon the quality time we spend with each other. I have acted upon my belief that human interaction is important. I believe there are some ideas in life that every person must ingest, understand, and act upon.

It is so important to thoroughly digest the ideas in this chapter. I want people to understand cancer and precisely why it is such a slippery threat, but I also want to expose its weaknesses. My ability to fully understand these concepts is critical for me, too, because it shapes my views on cancer therapies. It helps me to assess their potential and their weaknesses.

George Orwell, the author of the great anti-Stalinist novel *Animal Farm* said that "In times of universal deceit, telling the truth becomes a revolutionary act." Well, in regard to cancer, there is no shortage of deceit from both the alternative and orthodox medical establishments. I want to establish some straightforward truths that encourage revolutionary thinking.

The Strengths of Cancer

The first truth is that cancer is extremely resilient. Have you ever battled weeds in the spring? I've watched my neighbor stare down a patch of clover, armed like an old-time gunslinger, bottles of weed killer dangling from the trigger-happy fingers of both hands. I've watched him laugh maniacally as he blasted herbicide in every conceivable nook and cranny of his yard and front walk. I've also watched him several days later shaking his head at brand new patches of weeds.

Underestimating cancer's resilience is a mistake often made by proponents of alternative therapies who offer treatments that may be theoretically and scientifically sound but that are insufficient for the task at hand. However, the same mistake is often made by proponents of orthodox therapies who cite impressive scientific data touting the significant achievements in the war against cancer but who often find themselves offering only prospects of doom and gloom to their patients. It is a mistake to underestimate the resilience of cancer.

Cancer is a formidable foe because it is such an elusive target. Its strength resides in its "genetic instability."[2] Consider this for a moment. Every time a normal cell needs to replicate, it passes exact copies of a 3-billion-letter DNA code to each and every daughter cell. Now, the odds of a gene transmission error, commonly called a mutation, occurring are very high. Indeed, they happen all the time. However, the body has mechanisms to correct mutations.[3] For instance, cells are equipped with genes that suppress mutations. In addition, our immune system destroys mutated cells.

When these corrective mechanisms fail, cancerous cells develop. All cancers begin with a single mutated cell, which causes a cascade of mutations that result in a group of aberrant cells. Because the DNA of a mutated cell is unstable, cancer cells continue to mutate as they rapidly grow. The constant mutation means that the cancer the doctor treated yesterday may not be the same as the cancer he treats today and that cancer may not be the same as the cancer he will treat tomorrow.

From the very beginning, the medical community has chosen a very aggressive approach to the treatment of cancer.

Did you know that the first chemotherapy was developed after World War II when research on mustard gas demonstrated that it has the ability to kill rapidly dividing cells, like those found in the intestinal tract, bone marrow, and lymphatic system? [4] Mustard gas is extremely toxic however. Remember, it was developed for chemical warfare; not for medicinal use. Right from the onset, chemotherapy's biggest challenge has been the ratio of benefit to risk. Sometimes the benefit is greater than the risk, but usually it's the other way around.

In 1971, President Nixon teamed with the National Cancer Institute and, in his famous State of the Union speech, officially declared "War on Cancer" and instituted the National Cancer Act.[5] The goal was to develop a cure in ten years. In the decade that followed, chemotherapy scored impressive hits. There was evidence of dramatic cures and an increase in longevity for patients with some cancers. Here is the list of those cancers and the percentage of chemotherapeutic effectiveness: [6]

- Choriocarcinoma, 90%
- Burkitt's lymphoma (Stage I), 90%
- Testicular carcinoma (Stage II-III), 70-90%
- Childhood sarcomas (w/ radiation & surgery), 70-90%
- Nodular mixed lymphoma, 75%
- Childhood lymphomas, 75%
- Diffuse histiocytic lymphoma, 70%
- Acute lymphocytic leukemia, 60%
- Hodgkin's disease (Stage III and IV), 60%

A very impressive record, indeed! In fact, whenever I encounter a patient with one of these cancers, I quickly recommend the chemotherapy protocol that has yielded those results. Unfortunately, many of these cancers are quite rare. After the exciting results in that first decade, chemotherapy's success has seemed to stagnate.

In regard to the most common forms of cancer (lung, breast, prostate, colon, stomach, pancreas, bladder, ovary, head, neck, etc.), which account for close to 90% of cancer deaths in the industrialized world, clinicians tend to agree that chemotherapy is of little help.

Dr. Ulrich Abel, was a cancer biostatistician from the University of Heidelberg, Germany. He spent over a decade evaluating the published results for thousands of patients with a variety of common cancers who were treated with all kinds of chemotherapy protocols. In his seminal book *Chemotherapy of Advanced Epithelial Cancer*, Abel found that for "most of today's common solid cancers, the ones that cause 90% of the cancer deaths each year, chemotherapy has never proven to do any good at all." [7]

In 1991, a renowned American scientist raised a red flag as well. Dr. Albert Braverman is Professor of Hematology and Oncology at the State University of New York. He said that no solid tumor which was incurable in 1976 became curable by 1991. In an article published in *Lancet* titled "Medical Oncology in the 1990s," he wrote that "the time has come to cut back on the clinical investigation of new chemotherapeutic regimens for cancer and to cast a critical eye on the way chemotherapeutic treatment is now being administered." [8]

A few years earlier, in 1986, Dr. John Bailar III expressed his concerns. Working at the School of Public Health at Harvard, he carefully evaluated the national cancer program and said that the "...cancer program is in big trouble." He concluded in an article published in The New England Journal of Medicine that "...some 35 years of intense effort focused on improving treatment must be judged as a qualified failure." [9]

John Bailar III is no ordinary scientist. He has authored or co-authored more than 200 scientific articles and is the author or editor of 12 books, including *Medical Uses of Statistics*, a standard text for students in that specialty. [10] Bailar has received numerous awards for his work.

He is a former MacArthur fellow, a member of the National Academy of Sciences' Institute of Medicine and a fellow of the American Association for the Advancement of Science. He worked at the National Cancer Institute from 1956 to 1980. He was Editor-in-Chief of the Journal of the National Cancer Institute and has been on the Editorial Board of Cancer Research, and the New England Journal of Medicine. I could list other accomplishments. Suffice it to say, he is a heavy-hitter.

In 1990, the director of the National Cancer Institute, Samuel Broder, faced mounting pressure to explain the lackluster results of almost two decades of chemotherapeutic practice. He said that "...although we are still searching for answers, the hallmark of the 1990s will be the application of research results from the 1980s." [11]

To date, researchers have published more than 1.5 million research papers about cancer, some indicating practical applications of chemotherapy. [12] Yet, widespread disillusionment with chemotherapy continues to increase, even within the inner circle of orthodoxy. In 2007, the American Cancer Society stated in its prestigious yearly publication *Cancer Facts & Figures*, and I quote, "Surgery, radiation therapy, and chemotherapy... seldom produce a cure." [13]

Yet, if you read the medical journals specializing in cancer you'll find that many of the more than 1.5 million articles are about chemotherapy. Even more surprising is the fact that the bulk of the studies report success. These articles cite successes in petri dishes, Guinea pigs, and even with patients in controlled clinical trials. Meanwhile, in the real world of the cancer wards around the world, patients are dying at ever increasing rates.

Strengths and Weaknesses of Chemotherapy

Not all the news is bad. In 2006, the Centers for Disease Control and Prevention reported that the five-year survival rate for cancer patients improved from 50% in 1971 to 63% in 2003. [14] Chemotherapy may have played some role in this success, but the data is insufficient to credit chemotherapy alone for such a boost. Chemotherapy has been shown to increase the longevity of patients with a number of cancers. Chemotherapy may extend the lives of patients with ovarian cancer for years. It may prolong the lives of patients with high-grade non-Hodgkin's lymphoma or localized cancer of the small intestines, but more often than not the effect is a modest increase of only a few months.

According to a report published in the British Medical Journal about the efficacy of carboplatin and cisplatin produced by Bristol Myers, a major manufacturer of chemotherapeutic drugs, only 11% of patients taking carboplatin and only 15% of patients taking cisplatin had a total response to the drugs. In the cases studied, the patients experienced remission for an average of a year and survived an average of only two years. [15]

Many statisticians criticize the vast majority of studies that tout the efficacy of chemotherapy because the data is woefully insufficient to make such claims. In fact, the only tumors for which there is solid evidence indicating a benefit of chemotherapy are small-cell lung cancer and, to a lesser degree, non-small cell lung cancer. Unfortunately, the "benefit" translates into an average gain in longevity of three months. [16]

With successes like these, one need not wonder why the search for alternatives is so widespread. Yet, the world still waits for any alternative that solves the riddle of cancer. At the Oasis of Hope we have been testing non-toxic natural cures for a long time. We've tested the Rife Machine, hyperthermia, the Gerson diet, insulin therapy, and many others. Some of these therapies yielded no substantive benefit in controlled studies, but others, like natural cytotoxic agents, presented remarkable benefits for patients suffering from lung, prostate, breast, colon, and other common cancers.

Yet, it would be far-fetched to construe our results as breakthroughs because the data is insufficient to make such claims. We have tried to conduct by-the-book clinical research, but double-blind studies are virtually impossible to conduct in a modest private hospital. Even when we compare our stats against similar studies published in medical literature, our comprehensive approach clashes with the one-drug evaluations of other studies. Within the industry, there is little incentive to research un-patentable products when it costs a manufacturer close to $800 million US dollars simply to gain approval for a product.[17] For these reasons, justified or not, to date there are no definitive statistics, ours or otherwise, proving any alternative as "effective." Thankfully, the handful of "scientific" reports claiming to prove the ineffectiveness of several alternative therapies are quite biased and poorly conducted. These reports unravel upon careful examination.

I'll continue to rest on the strength of a simple argument. Alternative therapies, in contrast with chemotherapy, do not provoke suffering in general. I will continue to champion alternative therapies until such time as comprehensive clinical research generates sufficient data to convince me that a particular therapy is not "effective." This begs a very important question: What is the definition of effective?

How is Effectiveness Defined?

To the cancer research community, effectiveness is defined by the difference in tumor load before and after therapy. Tumor load refers to the number of cancer cells, the size of a tumor, or the amount of cancer in the body. If the tumor load decreases, then the therapy is deemed effective. Simple enough. Except, this definition does not in any way consider the bottom line for patients: Will the therapy halt the progression of the disease and significantly prolong my life?

To the manufacturers of chemotherapeutic drugs, effectiveness is defined by the FDA, which deems an effective chemotherapeutic agent as one which achieves a 50% or more reduction in tumor size for 28 days. [18] Again, does this definition assess whether the therapy can halt the progression of the disease and significantly prolong life? No.

To the oncologist effectiveness is defined by the degree to which a therapy can be endorsed without fear of legal repercussion. Therefore, no treatment is truly effective, and all too often oncologists present the worst case scenario.

There are other ill-defined terms in regard to cancer. The terms response, remission, and cure are rarely explained clearly to patients. The term "response" refers to tumor shrinkage. A total response is when the tumor disappears completely, a partial response is when the tumor is reduced by at least 50%, and a failed response is when the tumor is reduced by anything less than 50%. The term "remission" refers to the time period a response lasts. The term "cure" refers to a total response with a remission lasting 5 consecutive years; in some cancers, the remission has to last 10 years. This is certainly not the common understanding of the term "cured." Why are these terms so ill-defined?

Why? There are two cancer worlds. There is the world populated by the cancer research community, and there is the world populated by clinical oncologists and their patients. In the world of the research community, evaluating cancer is so difficult that researchers had to come up with a flexible and forgiving terminology such as "response," "remission," and "cure."

However, in the world populated by clinical oncologists and their patients, these terms are not always helpful. When a cancer patient talks with an oncologist, they want to know what the chances are that the chemotherapy they receive will 1) Halt the progression of the disease, 2) Prolong their life significantly, and 3) Secure quality of life for them. Unfortunately, oncologists often frame their responses in a language that is unequivocally unforgiving because oncologists in the "trenches" live with the fact that chemotherapy usually doesn't truly cure cancer, extend life significantly, or improve the quality of a patient's life.

Did you know that more Americans have died from cancer than have perished in all of the wars America has participated in put together starting from the Revolution through Iraq and Afghanistan? Did you know that after spending more than 250 billion dollars the death rate from cancer is virtually the same in 2008 as it was when the war on cancer began in 1971? In fact the current death rate from cancer is the same as it was in 1950. John C. Bailar, MD sadly paints the most accurate picture, "We have given it our best effort for decades: billions of dollars of support, the best scientific talent available. It hasn't paid off." [19]

I have written on this subject for years and I still feel that chemotherapy, if it is used as the primary weapon in the fight against cancer, is wrong and generally bad for the patient. So, why then am I writing a chapter called "The Case for Chemotherapy?" Oh, you're curious now, aren't you?

The Facts

Let me play hard-to-get for just a few more moments, while we look at three undeniable facts: 1) Chemotherapy tears down tumors fast, 2) Cancer cells mutate in ways that make them resistant to chemotherapy, and 3) Chemotherapy is toxic and causes serious side effects.

First, chemotherapy tears down tumors fast, much faster that any non-toxic therapy available. No one can argue with that fact. Oasis of Hope has offered chemotherapy as a seconda... weapon, to be used in cases of emergency only, since my father founded the hospital in 1963. When a patient's life is threatened because of the sheer size of a tumor or because a tumor is located in a deadly location, for example, blocking the main airway, then what is most important is to save the patient's life. If the patient does not have the luxury of time, then we will recommend chemotherapy because a non-toxic therapy will take a couple of months to reduce tumor size. It is only in these cases, where the risk to benefit ratio favors chemotherapy, that we will make this recommendation. In other words, we ask the following question, "Is the tumor more deadly than the chemotherapy?" If the answer is "yes," then we will always recommend the therapy! If the patient survives the chemotherapy, then we have a patient with the luxury of time who will benefit from natural and non-toxic therapies.

Second, cancer cells mutate in ways that make them resistant to chemotherapy. It is important to note that not all chemotherapeutic drugs are created equal. There are many differences but for the sake of this discussion I will group them by their level of toxicity, from mild to extreme. Oncologists will almost always start with the least aggressive chemotherapeutic drug to minimize negative side effects for the patient.

It is fair to say that most patients will "respond" to the mildly toxic chemotherapeutic drugs during the first round of treatment. Unfortunately, if the tumor comes back, which happens more frequently than oncologists would like, the cells have often developed a resistance to the previously used drug. Cancer cells develop resistance through a number of different adaptability mechanisms which render the formerly effective treatment ineffective. What is even more disturbing is that the stress caused by the therapy often causes the cancer cells to mutate in ways that render them more aggressive and difficult to treat. For example, a mildly toxic chemotherapeutic drug may destroy 99% of a moderately aggressive cancer, but the 1% of the cancer that

...nerapy often mutates into a highly aggressive ...ger responds to mildly toxic drugs. This is why ...ers have had to develop a second and third line of ...utic drugs, with each new line presenting an increase in . ...nd dangerous side effects.

...ird, chemotherapy is toxic and causes serious side effects. Tolerance to the toxic effects of chemotherapy varies from patient to patient. Some people die from exposure to the least aggressive drugs and other people experience zero adverse reactions to drugs that are so toxic that even those administering treatment are advised to wear rubber gloves. Some drugs cause nausea, vomiting, hair loss, muscle mass loss, blood disorders, heart damage, and lung damage. Others cause nerve damage, kidney damage, hearing loss, seizures, loss of motor function, bone marrow suppression, anemia, and blindness.

A most dreaded complication is mucositis, which is an inflammation of the mucus membranes in the mouth and stomach lining. Mucositis can lead to life-threatening diarrhea and bleeding. Some chemotherapeutic drugs can destroy bile ducts, cause bone tissue death, restrict growth, cause infertility, lower white and red cell counts, and lead to intestinal and lactose malabsorption. For these reasons, I will never support the use of chemotherapy as a palliative, which is a treatment designed to improve the patient's quality of life. Such an endorsement would certainly ignore the terrible effects which deteriorate a patient's quality of life. Again, why then am I writing a chapter called "The Case for Chemotherapy?"

I'm writing this chapter because of some important questions. What if there were ways to 1) Leverage the cancer killing potential of chemotherapy, 2) Re-sensitize resistant tumors to mildly toxic chemotherapeutic drugs, and 3) Protect healthy cells from the onslaught of chemotherapy thus reducing side effects to a minimum?

New and exciting studies published in mainstream medical journals are making me reevaluate my position on chemotherapy and consider this treatment from a new perspective and with an open mind. Researchers in the U.S. and abroad are reporting that, through cancer cell signaling transduction, a number of nutrients can effectively counter a cancer cell's resistance mechanisms. In practical terms, this means that it is possible to use first line chemotherapeutic drugs over and over again, because it is now possible to re-sensitize cancers to these drugs with lower toxicity levels.

Not only that, more and more research is demonstrating that it is possible to protect normal tissues and internal organs from the negative and destructive effects of chemotherapy.[20] How? With nutrients! The medicinal power of nutrients is a reality alternative oncologists have championed for decades. The difference is that these alternative practitioners are now recognized as highly qualified physicians. Many are fully accredited within the orthodox medical establishment. In addition, their work is now being published in peer-reviewed journals.

New and Effective Use of Chemotherapy

How do we use chemotherapy at the Oasis of Hope? This is a loaded question because chemotherapy is a very broad term. Chemotherapy is an anti-cancer therapy that uses cytotoxic drugs to kill cancer cells. There is an incredibly vast array of cytotoxic drugs and an infinite number of ways of combining and administering them. The precise treatment administered will depend on a number of variables including 1) The type of cancer, 2) The stage of development, 3) The physical status of the patient, 4) The prior chemotherapy treatments received, 5) The response to prior treatment, 6) The likelihood that negative side effects would eliminate the possibility of further treatment, and many other factors. This is why medical doctors specialize in the use of these very potent and dangerous drugs.

Suffice it to say, Oasis of Hope employs oncologists who specialize in chemotherapy. We thoroughly evaluate each patient in order to "tailor" the treatment in regard to 1) Drug, 2) Dosage, and 3) Duration. What separates our chemotherapy protocols from those around the world are two things. First, is the preparation our patients undergo to enhance the cancer-killing effect of the chemotherapy. Second, is the umbrella of protection we create over our patients that is designed to reduce negative side effects. You will read much more in the following chapters about the therapies we use that work together to overcome the failings of chemotherapy.

Many patients come to us in despair, their lives threatened, riddled with resistant tumors, often sent home to die because in the conventional worldview, nothing more can be done. I believe that "While there is life, there is hope…" as John Gay masterfully wrote in his 17th Century novel *The Sick Man and the Angel*. An opponent like cancer demands respect and disciplined research.

Given the wealth of new and exciting research, we must be ready to boldly consider revolutionary new approaches to cancer treatment with an open mind and be prepared to make therapeutical adjustments when new approaches are supported by convincing scientific evidence. More importantly, as we evaluate the effectiveness of these new and exciting therapies, we must ensure that our primary criteria is, in fact, the bottom line for patients. Do the therapies significantly slow the progression of the disease, significantly extend the life of the patient, and secure quality of life for the patient?

This is so important because much of the medical community is still entrenched in thinking that deems a treatment effective, or successful, merely because it reduces the size of the tumor. There are many treatments that shrink tumors but that do not extend the life of the patient, or secure quality of life for the patient. That is not success. It is a meaningless success at best. Sure, the tumor shrunk but the patient died.

Likewise, there are many in the medical community that would deem a treatment ineffective, or a failure, merely because it does not result in the significant reduction of the tumor. There are treatments that do not significantly shrink tumors, but that extend the life of the patient, and secure quality of life for the patient. That is not failure. It is a meaningful success. While the tumor may still exist, the patient continues to thrive for years. In my years of experience working with people who live with cancer, I have found that people will always choose to live strong even if cancer continues to be present, rather than pleasing the oncology establishment with a successful treatment that does not add any time to their lives.

This whole concept became crystal clear to me when I accompanied my father to a prestigious cancer treatment center in New York to review his cases. My dad put a number of X-rays up for review but the oncologists were confused if not annoyed. My dad's patients still had tumors. One oncologist said, "Your treatment has failed! The patient still has a tumor. Let me show you one of my patient's X-rays." The oncologist put up before and after films and explained, "See, the tumor is gone. Now that is success." My father exclaimed, "That is wonderful! How is the patient now?" The oncologist replied, "The patient died soon after treatment." My father stated, "My patient is still alive after five years even though there is some cancer left." The oncologist said, "That is still a failure."

This experience with my father helped me redefine our treatment goals. Tumor destruction would no longer be sufficient. We would fight to help our patients live longer and stronger.

Caleb Dominguez

Chemotherapy can be successful for a while. After a recurrence, a new chemo protocol often is also successful, and even for a third time it can be of help. But some patients get to the point where their body will no longer withstand chemotherapy. Caleb had such a predicament; obviously, stopping chemo was a death sentence in his case. Through our preconditioning oxidative stress therapy, and the rest of our IRT, we were able to send him back to his oncologists to begin chemo again. This is what happened...

- Dr. Contreras

"Essentially the decision to go to Oasis of Hope was the last option we had. We weren't too sure about this place. We were very hesitant and anxious. We weren't sure what to expect. However, we had heard a lot of good things, from close friends, church families, neighbors and long time friends, that there was something different about Oasis of Hope. That's when things started turning around.

I feel great right now, I feel that I have my strength back and that I'm getting back to my routine in life. I want to go back to college, I want to use this experience that I've had and share it because I have high expectations for my life, and I know that some people lose hope. This past year gave me something to work for. In my life, this whole experience was a miracle. In the very beginning there was no hope and now I'm ready to go back to school, I am ready to get back to my life and to do more things that I ever expected.

There was a point during my initial treatment where the cancer started to get much worse. My symptoms weren't improving, and I wasn't tolerating chemotherapy as much as I should have. So we came to a point after a few months of receiving radiation and chemotherapy where I was too weak. We came to a point where my doctors were telling us that my case wasn't very hopeful. I went to Oasis of Hope and began a whole different style of treatment.

I immediately noticed a complete difference in the way I felt. My initial experience was totally different than what my family or I initially expected. In February 2006, a MRI, spinal tap and bone marrow biopsy all concluded that the cancer was gone. At Oasis of Hope I never had a symptom or was in pain. It was 100% different and I was glad to have decided to go the Oasis of Hope and experience how different the environment is. There's always hope, there's hope for everybody. Put your trust in God. Once you believe you can overcome this disease, you start believing that there's always hope."

Caleb Dominguez
San Diego, California
USA

71

6

Traffic signals save lives. Mixed signals spawn chaos.

Regulating Healthy Cell Behavior

Joe the accountant was a man of order and balance. He developed a highly regulated existence. He identified with Olympic swimming champion Michael Phelps, who declared that his life was summed up by eating, swimming, and sleeping. Joe kept his regimen, of eating, crunching numbers, and sleeping, on track by automated reminders  from his Blackberry-PDA that was synched with his desktop PC. Day in and day out, Joe the accountant would conduct his daily duties with discipline and on occasion he would deviate, by order of his Blackberry, and take his wife out for their anniversary or celebrate his child's birthday. These little prompts would change Joe's normal behavior for the special task he would need to perform, and then he would return to his regular activities. The only other thing he did outside of numbers was to volunteer as a firefighter. He would receive a Blackberry fire alert about once every two months and he would immediately drop everything to go put out the fire.

To say that Joe the accountant was predictable was pretty accurate. Aside from his firefighting duties, you would know exactly what he was doing at any given moment. But, one day, Joe mistakenly thought he received a Blackberry fire alert. He rushed to the station but was sent home. The next day it happened two more times. On the third day, Joe rushed down to the station eight times without ever receiving stimulus from his Blackberry. His PDA no longer regulated his behavior. He was sent home each of the eight times, but he unexpectedly returned a ninth time, suited up, and took a fire truck to a random address. He connected the big fire hose, wet down the whole house, and broke down the front door with an ax yelling, "I am here to rescue you!" There was no fire. He went to jail for stealing government property, as well as breaking and entering. His behavior was inexplicably altered and he was considered to be dangerous. Joe had gone rogue.

Much like Joe, the behavior of our body's cells is tightly regulated to insure that each cell acts in a way that supports the health of the whole body. But acquired alterations of a cell's genetic material can disrupt the intricate internal mechanisms that govern cell behavior, causing the cell to multiply and spread in ways that are detrimental or even lethal to the body. A cell that behaves like this is just like Joe; it has gone rogue – and that's what we call cancer.

Over the last several decades, molecular biology has gradually been unraveling the way in which the body's cells work. "Signal transduction" refers to the way in which cellular proteins undergo small and usually reversible changes in their structure to induce alterations in cell behavior. The genetic material of cancer cells is typically altered in ways that over activate intracellular signal transduction mechanisms, specifically, the ones related to the malignant behavior of cancer. Some of these mechanisms prevent the process of apoptosis (programmed cell death) as well as support cellular multiplication, tissue invasion and metastasis (the spread of cancer to distant organs), and the resistance to being killed by chemotherapy or radiation. Cell Signal Transduction Therapy seeks to regulate the signaling pathways in cancer cells to make them kill and control.

One of the goals at Oasis of Hope is to use nutrients, phytochemicals (natural chemicals derived from plants), and currently available drugs to suppress signal transduction pathways that are overactive in cancer cells, or boost pathways that are under active. This will help make cancer cells easier to kill while suppressing their capacity to grow, spread to distant organs, and evoke the growth of new blood vessels that feed tumors.

The nutrients, phytochemicals, and safe drugs we use in the Cell Signal Transduction Therapy include among others omega-3 fatty acids from fish oil, silibinin, green tea extract, boswellic acids, salsalate, diclofenac, and disulfiram.

Some of the Signaling Pathways Overactivated in Cancer Cells

One the signaling pathways that is chronically overactive in many cancers is known as "NF-kappaB." This protein complex regulates the synthesis of a number of other proteins by binding to DNA in the cellular nucleus. In a high proportion of advanced cancers, NF-kappaB is either continuously activated or is rapidly activated in response to chemotherapy.[1-5] One of the most important roles of NF-kappaB is to boost the production of a number of proteins that act in a variety of ways to prevent the process of apoptosis.[6] This is the "cell suicide" process that is the most common way in which cytotoxic anti-cancer drugs kill cancer cells. Moreover, NF-kappaB also increases production of a "multidrug resistance" membrane protein that functions to "pump" various cytotoxic chemicals, including many anti-cancer drugs, out of cells.[7] For these reasons, NF-kappaB activation, either chronic, or triggered by chemotherapy, tends to protect cancer cells during chemotherapy. Conversely, many studies show that inhibitors of NF-kappaB activity can make resistant cancer cells much more sensitive to chemotherapy and/or radiation.[8-11]

Chronic activation of NF-kappaB also makes cancers act more aggressively. This results in increased production of "angiogenic factors" that promote the development of new blood vessels required for cancer growth, increased production of proteolytic enzymes (enzymes which break down proteins) which enable cancer cells to penetrate and migrate through tissues, and increased production of certain factors that promote rapid cellular multiplication.[12]

The bottom line is that cancers, which have evolved high NF-kappaB activity, tend to spread more rapidly and aggressively, and they are harder to kill off. As if NF-kappaB weren't already pernicious enough for cancer patients, this factor is now known to be a key mediator of the muscle protein loss associated with cancer cachexia.[13] Thus, effective inhibition of NF-kappaB likely has the potential to help cancer patients preserve their muscle mass.

Another factor which is overactivated in many cancers is the enzyme "cyclooxygenase-2," more conveniently referred to as "Cox-2." This enzyme, which is continuously active, generates a group of hormone-like compounds known as prostanoids, many of which have inflammatory and pain-promoting activity. That's why inhibitors of Cox-2 are frequently used to treat inflammatory conditions. However, some of the prostanoids produced by Cox-2 in cancer cells have growth factor activity for these cancers.[14] This growth factor activity promotes increased cancer proliferation, boosts angiogenesis, and also can make cancers harder to kill.[15-19] Furthermore, some prostanoids have local immunosuppressive activity that blunts the effectiveness of immune cells that attack the tumor.[20]

It should be noted that both NF-kappaB and Cox-2 play a direct role in angiogenesis. Activation of these factors occurs in endothelial cells – the cells that give rise to new blood vessels during the angiogenic process. Angiogenesis is required for efficient production of new blood vessels.[21-23] Thus, inhibition of these proteins has the potential to directly suppress angiogenesis by targeting endothelial cell function.

Another enzyme expressed by many cancer cells that promotes cancer growth and survival is "5-lipoxygenase" ("5-LPO"). This enzyme induces production of pro-inflammatory compounds known as "leukotrienes." Just like the prostanoids produced by Cox-2, leukotrienes can promote the growth and survival of certain cancers – including many which have 5-LPO activity.[24-26] Inhibiting 5-LPO typically retards the growth of cancer cell lines dependent on 5-LPO, and often increases the rate at which these cells die by apoptosis. Human cancer cell lines derived from prostatic, pancreatic, breast, esophageal, colorectal, bladder, gastric, and renal cancers, as well as mesotheliomas and leukemias, have shown 5-LPO dependency.[27-34] Not all such cancers are 5-LPO dependent.

Another overactive signaling pathway in many cancer cells is triggered by over expression of the "epidermal growth factor receptor" (EGF-R). Cancers which express EGF-R also will usually make hormones that can activate this receptor, or have enzymatic activities that can activate it from within the cell, bypassing the need for hormonal activation. Activated EGF-R, like other growth factor receptors, promotes the proliferation and spread of cancer cells, while suppressing the cell death mechanism, apoptosis, that enables chemotherapy drugs to kill cancer cells.

Another key growth factor produced by many cancers is "vascular endothelial growth factor" (VEGF). Although VEGF has growth factor activity for some cancers, its more important role in cancer spread is to promote angiogenesis by aiding the multiplication and survival of the endothelial cells that form the new blood vessels required for cancer growth. The Oasis of Hope IRT regimens seek to interfere with this process by either suppressing tumor production of VEGF, or by blocking the receptors in endothelial cells that enable them to respond to VEGF. One of the ways in which NF-kappaB and EGF-R promote cancer spread is by boosting tumor production of VEGF and certain other angiogenic growth factors.

Now let's take a look at some of the agents – nutrients, phytochemicals, and safe drugs – which the Oasis of Hope IRT regimens employ to inhibit the overactive signaling pathways in cancer cells that promote cancer survival and spread.

Fish Oil

Fish oil is a uniquely rich source of the long-chain omega-3 fatty acids EPA (eicosapentaenoic acid) and DHA (docosahexaenoic acid). A small structural difference distinguishes these fatty acids from the omega-6 fatty acids found in plant-derived oils.

EPA and DHA have a valuable role to play in cancer treatment. A number of studies show that a diet rich in fish oil tends to slow tumor growth.[35-38] At least part of this effect can be attributed to a suppressive effect of fish oil on angiogenesis. Remember, angiogenesis is the process by which new blood vessels develop to enable the growth and spread of tumors.[37-40] EPA has been shown to decrease the expression of a key receptor in endothelial cells that makes them responsive to VEGF.[41]

Another key factor in angiogenesis is the enzyme Cox-2. In endothelial cells, it produces prostanoids required for vascular tube formation during the angiogenic process.[42] A high intake of fish oil has the potential to antagonize the role of Cox-2 in the angiogenic process by decreasing the production of Cox-2-derived prostanoids. It also may blunt the production of growth-promoting prostanoids in cancer cells.

Fish oil has the ability to fend off cachexia, the severe loss of muscle mass that often complicates late-stage cancer.[43-46] Although cachexia usually entails a loss of appetite that can contribute to weight loss by decreasing calorie intake, the life-threatening selective loss of muscle mass often seen in cancer patients reflects a very specific inflammatory process in muscle fibers that is not seen in healthy dieters. It has been discovered that EPA interferes with the inflammatory mechanisms that cause loss of muscle mass.

Silibinin

Milk thistle extract has been used for many decades in the treatment of liver disorders. Approximately 80% of this extract consists of silymarin, a mixture of several compounds known as flavonolignans. Silibinin, the most prominent of these compounds, accounts for about 60% of the weight of silymarin, and is believed to be responsible for most of the liver-protective activity of silymarin and milk thistle extract. Just within the last decade, scientists have learned that silibinin has considerable potential for preventing and treating cancer.

In concentrations that may be feasible to achieve with high-dose clinical regimens, silibinin has been shown to have growth inhibitory effects on a wide range of human cancer cell lines including cancers arising from the prostate, breast, colon, lung, liver, bladder, and cervix.[47-54] Silibinin can suppress the proliferation of these cells, while at the same time increasing the rate at which they die by apoptosis. In addition, silibinin can sensitize cancer cell lines to the killing effects of certain cytotoxic chemotherapeutic drugs.[55] Thus, silibinin may have potential both for retarding the growth and spread of cancer and for boosting the response of cancers to chemotherapy.

The mechanisms responsible for these effects have been studied most intensively in human prostate cancer cells.[56] It should first be noted that these studies show that concentrations of silibinin, which retard the growth of these prostate cancers, do not influence the growth of healthy normal prostate cells. In other words, the effects of silibinin on cell proliferation appear to be specific to cancer cells. The anti-proliferative effects of silibinin on prostate cancer cells have been traced to decreased function of the epidermal growth factor receptor (EGF-R). This is a key mediator of growth signals in prostate cancer and in many other types of cancer.[57] Silibinin binds to this receptor and prevents it from interacting with hormones that activate it – some of which are produced by prostate cancers. Furthermore, silibinin induces prostate cancer cells to make more of a compound, known as IGFBP-3, that binds to and inhibits the activity of insulin-like growth factor-I (IGF-I), a key growth factor for many cancers.[58] IGF-I is produced by the liver and circulates in the blood, where it acts to promote tissue growth throughout the body. In addition, some cancers can make their own IGF-I.

As if these benefits weren't enough, silibinin has also been shown to suppress the NF-kappaB signaling pathway. The effect of silibinin on NF-kappaB helps to rationalize silibinin's ability to increase the sensitivity of cancers to certain chemotherapy drugs. The effects of silibinin on EGF-R, which likewise promotes cancer cell survival, also contribute in this regard.

The impact of orally administered silibinin on the growth of human tumors in immunodeficient mice has been studied with three different types of tumors – prostate, lung, and ovarian.[59, 60] In each case, silibinin has been found to have a substantial and dose-dependent suppressive effect on tumor growth in doses that had no apparent toxicity to the treated animals.

Examination of the silibinin-treated tumors revealed that they had a much less developed vasculature than control tumors. In other words, there were less blood vessels in the tumor to provide nourishment and oxygen.[59, 60] Follow-up studies showed that in some cancers silibinin could suppress secretion of the pro-angiogenic factor VEGF. Furthermore, other studies show that clinically feasible concentrations of silibinin have a direct effect on endothelial cells. Silibinin can suppress the proliferation of these cells and reduce their ability to migrate, invade tissues, and roll themselves into tubes, which is how new blood vessels are formed.[61,62] These findings suggest that the growth-slowing impact of silibinin on tumors reflects the interaction of at least three phenomena: a direct anti-proliferative effect on cancer cells; a suppression of VEGF production by these cells; and a direct inhibitory effect on the capacity of endothelial cells to build new blood vessels. Silibinin deserves a gold medal!

Green Tea Extract

The green tea extract employed at Oasis of Hope is highly potent. It comprises 98% polyphenols, the most prominent of which is the compound epigallocatechin-gallate, better and more conveniently known as "EGCG." Some of the first studies evaluating strategies for suppressing angiogenesis showed that oral administration of green tea could slow angiogenesis in mice. More recently, research shows that clinically achievable concentrations of EGCG can achieve partial inhibition of the receptor in endothelial cells that responds to VEGF. (This receptor, or the VEGF that activates it, is targeted by several new hyper-expensive cancer drugs that target the bioactivity of VEGF.) The strategy employed by Oasis of Hope is to attack angiogenesis from as many angles as feasible, in the hope that the cumulative effect will be a clinically worthwhile retardation of tumor growth.[63-66]

Boswellic Acids

Boswellic acids are a group of closely related compounds found in salai guggul, a resinous extract from the tree Boswellia carteri, that is traditionally used in Ayurvedic (Indian) medicine as an anti-inflammatory agent.[67] In the early 1990s, German researchers discovered the mechanistic basis for salai guggul's anti-inflammatory efficacy. Boswellic acids are very potent inhibitors of the enzyme 5-LPO – and thus can suppress production of leukotrienes which act as cancer growth factors.

The impact of 5-LPO activity on the sensitivity of cancers to chemotherapy or radiotherapy has received little attention up to this point. However, one fascinating recent report indicates that, concurrent expression of 5-LPO is associated with substantial protection from the cytotoxicity of chemotherapeutic cancer drugs.[68] Conversely, suppression of 5-LPO in these cancers greatly enhances their sensitivity to these drugs. This implies that 5-LPO inhibitors, administered prior to and during chemotherapy, should enhance the responsiveness of a high proportion of human cancers.

Zileuton, is a drug that can inhibit 5-LPO and has shown cancer-retardant activity in hamsters with pancreatic cancer.[69] However, we have chosen to use boswellic acid-rich extracts in Oasis of Hope IRT regimens because they are considerably less expensive and can be presumed to be safe based on centuries of use in traditional medicine. Moreover, a number of cell culture studies indicate that boswellic acids, most notably one known as acetyl-11-keto-beta-boswellic acid, can slow the proliferation and boost the death rate of various human cancer cell lines.[70-74]

The only published clinical experience with boswellic acids in the treatment of cancer dealt with the use of these agents in children with progressing brain cancers.[75, 76] Although some of the children experienced improved neurological function during this treatment, this might have reflected an anti-inflammatory effect of leukotriene suppression rather than tumor regression. Nonetheless, the observed benefit was worthwhile. In rats transplanted with gliomas, treatment with boswellic acids could more than double survival time.[77] In the IRT protocol and at-home regimen, we include a potent dose of boswellic acids.

Salsalate

Fortunately, several drugs are available which can suppress the signaling pathways activated by either NF-kappaB or Cox-2. One of these is salicylic acid, a natural compound found in white willow bark that has been used for many decades to treat inflammatory disorders such as rheumatoid arthritis. In the late nineteenth century, German chemists first synthesized aspirin (acetylsalicylic acid) by adding an acetyl group to salicylic acid. Salicylic acid, like aspirin, can inhibit cyclooxygenase enzymes, but its activity in this regard is very weak and reversible. This explains why salicylic acid doesn't produce the dangerous side effects sometimes seen with chronic use of aspirin or related drugs, such as bleeding stomach ulcers or kidney damage.[78-80] It is now known that the anti-inflammatory effects of high-dose salicylic acid are more likely to reflect inhibition of NF-kappaB activation. Salicylic acid binds to and inhibits an enzyme that is usually required for NF-kappaB activation.[81, 82]

Although pharmaceutical companies are working feverishly to develop expensive new inhibitors of NF-kappaB, few medical scientists have considered the possibility of using natural, inexpensive salicylate in cancer therapy.[83] There is however recent research establishing that salicylate has cancer-retardant and anti-angiogenic activity. At Oasis of Hope, we believe that salicylic acid has considerable potential for use in cancer therapy, to potentiate the efficacy of chemotherapy in certain cancers, to slow the growth and spread of cancer during at-home therapy, and to slow or prevent the progression of cachexia muscle degeneration.[84, 85]

Several pharmaceutical forms of salicylic acid are available. We have chosen to use salsalate, a complex which is broken down in the intestinal tract to release free salicylic acid, which is then absorbed.[86] Salsalate is less likely to induce gastric irritation that other forms of salicylic acid. It was developed in Japan about 50 years ago, and has been in use since that time for treatment of inflammatory disorders. Salsalate won't produce dangerous toxicity when used as directed. However, in optimally effective anti-inflammatory doses, it can produce reversible ear dysfunction – tinnitus ("ringing in the ears") and mild hearing loss.[87] Fortunately, these problems resolve as soon as the drug is discontinued, and no permanent damage is done. For the occasional patient in whom these side effects are highly troubling, a dosage reduction can often solve the problem. It is necessary to use these high doses to achieve effective inhibition of NF-kappaB.

Diclofenac

With respect to Cox-2, there are many drugs, commonly referred to as NSAIDs, which can inhibit this enzyme. Some of these drugs are relatively selective to Cox-2 – including the prominently advertised drugs Vioxx and Celebrex. In other words, these drugs have little impact on the other form of cyclooxygenase (Cox-1). Prolonged effective inhibition of Cox-1 can lead to serious complications such as bleeding stomach ulcerations and kidney damage. For that reason, pharmaceutical companies developed Cox-2-specific inhibitors for use in the treatment of inflammatory disorders.

Instead of using the expensive, highly advertised and relatively new Cox-2-specific inhibitors Celebrex or Vioxx, we at Oasis of Hope have decided to use a much older drug, diclofenac. Diclofenac has an activity spectrum nearly identical to that of Celebrex, producing effective inhibition of Cox-2 in concentrations that only modestly impact Cox-1, but it is much less expensive.[88] When administered in standard clinical doses, diclofenac is more effective than Vioxx at inhibiting Cox-2 in the human body.[89] While diclofenac has recently been shown to increase heart attack risk like other Cox-2-specific inhibitors do,[90] we always use it in conjunction with low-dose aspirin, which likely will largely offset that risk.

Disulfiram

Another drug with potential for inhibiting NF-kappaB is disulfiram – the drug more commonly known as "Antabuse." This drug was developed many years ago to help alcoholics abstain from alcohol. If they drink alcohol while using Antabuse, they become ill, owing to increased blood levels of the alcohol metabolite acetaldehyde. More recently, it has been discovered that disulfiram can inhibit cellular components known as proteasomes.[91,92] Proteasomes are responsible for degrading cellular proteins which have been specifically targeted for degradation. They play a crucial role in the activation of NF-kappaB by degrading a protein that inhibits this activation. Thus, inhibition of proteasome function usually decreases NF-kappaB activity.[93] Recent studies show that disulfiram and related sulfur-containing compounds can inhibit proteasomes and thereby suppress NF-kappaB activity in cancer cells. This renders them less aggressive and more susceptible to eradication.[92] In usual clinical doses, disulfiram is a reasonably well tolerated drug as long as the patient does not drink any alcoholic beverage. The dose-limiting toxicity is gastrointestinal upset.

Conclusion

It is not likely that many oncologists discuss Signal Transduction with their patients. But most people facing cancer want to know what causes it. We can be sure that pollution, chemicals, diet, lack of exercise, and other important facts of the world we live in stress our bodies, even at the cellular level. Stressed cells sometimes undergo small and irreversible changes in their structures, which alter their behaviors. If these changes go uncontested, the cell can become unhealthy and mutate into a cancer cell which will begin to multiply, form a tumor, and then spread. Fortunately, research is uncovering information of how to re-regulate unhealthy cell's behaviors. Though the information in this chapter was a touch on the technical side, it is important for you to understand that the Oasis of Hope medical and scientific team is aware of this aspect of cancer, and it is using the scientifically supported agents that can help regulate cellular behavior.

Ken Papini

Oxidative stress by itself kills cancer cells. Kenneth Papini was told that he had such an aggressive cancer of the esophagus that no matter how much chemo or radiation therapy he would receive, he was going to die of this cancer. So, he chose not to have chemo. We offered autohematotherapy with ozone as sole oxidative stress therapy. Here is his story...

- Dr. Contreras

"I first went to the doctor after I noticed that I had difficulty swallowing. It really never occurred to me that it could be cancer. Quickly I was scheduled for surgery on November 16, 2004 after doctors found a tumor in my esophagus. It took me two months to recover after the first surgery. Unfortunately, the tumor had already spread to my lymph nodes and the doctors told me that I had stage III cancer. I was sent to an oncologist and he laid out a pretty grim report, stating that no matter what therapies they used, the cancer was going to come back and kill me. He told me I had no choice. After hearing that from my doctor, I decided to go to Oasis of Hope.

We arrived at Oasis of Hope in January of 2005, and I have been doing great ever since. It was my wife's idea for us to go to Oasis of Hope. She had had cancer in the 1970s and was a patient there, and Dr. Ernesto Contreras Sr. was her physician. All these years later, she is still cancer free. Linda is like having a doctor right with you, she knows everything about this disease, she knows everything about the diet, she is very supportive, she makes sure that I don't miss a pill, and she makes sure that I don't miss any kind of therapy that I am supposed to have. She is a constant reminder of what we're doing and she is a big supporter. I like the fact that Oasis of Hope encourages patients to come with companions.

I spent three weeks in the treatment center, and then came home on a Wednesday and was on the ski slopes on the sierra on a Friday. That was great and I felt wonderful. Not only did I ski, but also I was an active member for the full season of the men's senior baseball league. I played around twenty-two games and made the all-star team later that year. Given where I had been the year previously, it was quite an accomplishment. I got my strength back and was able to play baseball and actually ski, it was amazing. It's a blessing from God being strong and able to fight off the thoughts that creep into your head; especially when there are different pains that keep showing up. For example, a cough or soreness in your throat, you really have to battle through those kinds of things and believe that you're okay. A positive attitude is very important.

I think the most important thing is for people to realize what a special place Oasis of Hope is. It has a very special place in my heart. I keep in constant contact with them and I look forward to every six months when we make our return visits. I believe that the follow-up visits are a big part to the success of the therapy. They make staying connected with the treatment center real easy because it's just part of the therapy. On my last follow up visit in July 2005, I was declared to be in full remission. From then on my blood test and my CT scans have been excellent and I feel great."

Ken Papini
Sacramento, California
USA

7

Too much or too little are equally undesirable.

A Balance of Give and Take

Unless you have been living under a rock for the past decade, I am sure you have witnessed to some degree the surging video game craze. I don't even pretend to understand what's happening in the actual games. I just sit there slack-jawed as the kids annihilate some creature that is either huge, ugly, covered in slime, or all of the above. The most

Redox Regulatory Therapy

attractive feature of some modern video games is called "co-op mode," which allows players to cooperate on a team against an opponent controlled by the software. If you ever want a lesson in diplomacy, watch two kids playing a video game together in "co-op" mode. It is amazing to watch the live-time negotiation of give-and-take that occurs between the two as they attempt to secure team victory. Two kids will quickly determine each others' strengths and weaknesses and exploit that knowledge to their collaborative benefit. Give-and-take is the central principle of diplomacy. In a way, the principal of give-and-take is exactly what this chapter is all about. I will admit that the concept of oxidation and reduction is a bit confusing. However, I am confident I can "reduce" the concept to what is important and practical in regard to killing malignant cells.

Oxidation & Reduction

When chemists first discovered that iron reacts with oxygen and that the result of that interaction was corrosion, they named the process "oxidation." The name was understandable because scientists recognized the "give-and-take" principal in operation. They found that the air "gives" oxygen which the iron "takes" and that the end result is the production of rust. Substances that give away oxygen molecules are called oxidizing agents.

Likewise, when we remove rust and purify metal by removing the additional oxygen molecules, the process is called "reduction." Chemical agents that take up oxygen molecules are called reducing agents. Again, this is an over-simplified version of the oxidation and reduction concept, also know as "redox." This over-simplified version of the concept of redox, of rusting and un-rusting, is just too "rustic" for enlightened chemists. Scientists now know that redox happens far beyond the molecular level, it actually takes place at the atomic level.

Before we go any further, let me review the components of an atom. An atom consists of a dense central nucleus, which is composed of a mix of positively charged protons and electrically neutral neutrons. This nucleus is surrounded by a cloud of negatively charged electrons. It is the ratio of protons to electrons, which determines the "electrical state," or "oxidation state," of an atom. Under normal conditions, an atom contains an equal number of positive to negative charges so its "oxidation state" should be neutral.

This "electrical" balance is lost when the electron content of an atom is altered. The give-and-take of electrons determines the oxidative state of an atom. Oxidation occurs when an electrically neutral atom loses, or gives away, an electron. Conversely, reduction happens when an oxidative atom gains, or takes back, an electron, thus restoring electrical neutrality. A simple way to memorize this concept is to remember OIL RIG.

Oxidation Is Loss—Reduction Is Gain

Free Radicals

Electrons like company and, generally, you will find them in pairs. Agents that cause the loss of an electron are called "oxidants." These substances create an extremely unstable atom, because electrons need to be paired. An unstable atom with an unpaired electron is called a "free radical." These unstable atoms must resolve the instability in nanoseconds, so they do one of two things: 1) Take a electron from a neighboring atom to restore balance, or 2) Give up the unpaired electron to restore balance. Either way, in restoring balance within themselves "free radicals" upset the balance in neighboring cells. What follows is a chain reaction of oxidation and reduction.

I don't want you to think that free radicals are all bad. In fact, they can act as important mediators within the body. Often, they defend us from infectious agents. However, it is important to maintain a healthy give-and-take ratio in regard to free radicals. When an excess of oxidative agents persists, the result is molecular and cellular damage.

To counteract the chain reaction of oxidation and reduction caused by free radicals, the body has a host of antioxidant mechanisms to correct the problem. For example, there are electron-donor molecules, better known as "anti-oxidants," that can restore balance. The vitamins C and E are two such anti-oxidants. In addition, our body produces a number of enzymes that neutralize oxidation, such as superoxide dismutase, catalase, glutathione peroxidase, and thioreductase.

Yet, the mere presence of these protective mechanisms is not always enough because the real issue is the balance of give-and-take. When imbalance persists, either because of the excess production of free radicals, or because of the insufficient production of protective antioxidant mechanisms, free radical damage can get the upper hand. This is a condition known as "oxidative stress," which can cause serious cellular damage and result in the development of chronic-degenerative diseases like cancer.

Malignant cancer cells, because they are mutated, behave in really nasty ways. One thing they do is create an environment that serves to protect the tumor from the body's natural defense mechanisms and that promotes rapid growth. There are two important aspects of this cancer-friendly environment. The environment must maintain a constant and moderate level of oxidative-stress and low levels of oxygen. This environment makes it harder to kill the cancer and encourages the cancer to become aggressive.

Turning Cancer's Strength Into Its Weakness

Now comes the silver lining! The tendency of malignant cancer cells to create a cancer-friendly internal environment may seem like a strength on the surface. Except, this strength can be transformed into a weakness. This is because oxidative-stress environments are quite unstable. Therefore, a judo approach, which uses the supposed strength of an opponent against them, can turn the tables and transform this cancer-friendly environment into an anti-cancer environment.

You see, an environment that maintains a moderate amount of oxidative stress can precondition malignant tissues to neutralize the action of anti-oxidants produced by or introduced into the body. Yet, this environment does not prepare malignant tissues to deal with higher levels of oxidative stress. Creating an unbearable level of oxidative stress in the environment around malignant cells is the mechanism of a number of chemotherapeutic drugs use to destroy cancer. Unfortunately, these drugs are very toxic and damage healthy tissue, resulting in a range of unpleasant and dangerous side effects.

However, chemotherapeutic drugs are not the only substances that can effectively create unbearable levels of oxidative stress in the environment surrounding malignant cells. There are other less toxic oxidants that can achieve the same effect. One well-researched cancer-killing oxidant is hydrogen peroxide. In the past, a number of therapists administered high doses of hydrogen peroxide orally and intravenously, but the results were poor. This was because blood has anti-oxidant mechanisms to counteract oxidative stress. One of these mechanisms is the ability of red blood cells to produce generous amounts of an enzyme called catalase that efficiently breaks down hydrogen peroxide before it reaches the tissues.

Vitamin C: An Anti-tumor Agent

Researchers then discovered that a highly-concentrated dose of vitamin C is "selectively" toxic to cancer cells, meaning the high dose of vitamin C harms cancer cells but not healthy tissue. Yet, when this treatment was coupled with the addition of the enzyme catalase the cancer-killing effect of the treatment was reduced significantly. This led researchers to believe that the high dose vitamin C infusion resulted in the production of large quantities of hydrogen peroxide, which initially caused a cancer-killing effect that was then neutralized by the addition of the enzyme catalase. This suggested that cancer cells do not produce a sufficient amount of catalase to neutralize high levels of hydrogen peroxide on their own.

In fact, we now know that a large number of cancer cells produce small amounts of catalase in order to sustain low concentrations of hydrogen peroxide.[1-3] This creates the cancer-friendly environment of mild oxidative stress that encourages malignant cells to grow rapidly and become more aggressive.[4-7] Fortunately for everyone, because a high proportion of cancers are only able to produce small amounts of catalase, they are very vulnerable to the cancer-killing effect exhibited by high levels of hydrogen peroxide.

Dr. Mark Levine, an internationally acclaimed researcher at the National Institutes of Health, led a team of researchers to analyze the cancer-killing effect of high-dose vitamin C treatment. They discovered that after a high dose and rapid intravenous infusion of vitamin C, large concentrations of vitamin C can be reached in the extracellular space. There, vitamin C reacts spontaneously with the molecular oxygen within tumors and generates large amounts of hydrogen peroxide, which is lethal to tumor cells that produce only small amounts of catalase.[8, 9]

The irony here is astounding. For years, vitamin C has been recognized as one of the most powerful anti-oxidants available. How can a substance with anti-oxidant properties, produce levels of oxidative stress sufficient to kill cancer? The answer is simple. The effect of vitamin C within the body is dose dependent. In fact, there are many substances that render very different effects depending on the size of the dose. Do not forget that the difference between a venom and a cure is often in the amount. Hard to believe, but even drinking too much water can kill you.

Way back in the 1970's, the Nobel Prize winning scientist Dr. Linus Pauling collaborated with a British cancer surgeon, Ewan Cameron. They promoted the intravenous and oral administration of high-dose vitamin C treatment for terminal cancer patients. Pauling believed that anti-oxidant therapy was the way to kill cancer cells. In two published clinical trials they reported that patients significantly prolonged their lives and enjoyed an improved quality of life.

Pauling and Cameron used a megadose of 10 grams administered intravenously followed by an additional 10 grams administered orally! Many criticized him for such an irresponsible amount. In later years, C.G. Moertel conducted controlled clinical studies at the Mayo Clinic and reported in the New England Journal of Medicine that he was unable to replicate the results of Pauling and Cameron.

Many considered the case for high-dose vitamin C treatment closed. Nevertheless, thirty years later, researchers from the National Institutes of Health found it necessary to reopen the case in view of recent research. Mark Levine's team concluded that C.G. Moertel's studies failed because he only administered the vitamin C orally.

The research at the National Institutes of Health has proven that in order to consistently achieve the concentration of vitamin C sufficient to provoke oxidation, a patient must receive dozens of grams of intravenous infusions of vitamin C. Oral administration is completely ineffective in this regard.[10] A number of published case reports show that repeated high-dose intravenous vitamin C treatments yield objective tumor regression.[11-13] These case reports are so compelling that intravenous vitamin C therapy is currently being formally evaluated in clinical trials at the NIH.

In theory, high-dose vitamin C therapy should not cause toxic damage to healthy tissue because the body produces sufficient amounts of catalase to efficiently neutralize the hydrogen peroxide produced. Our experience in the real world certainly supports the theory. We have treated hundreds of patients in this manner with no side effects. Our current protocol insures blood and tissue levels of vitamin C that are safe and effective to kill cancer cells.

Yet, a burning question still remains. Why hasn't this therapy worked for everyone? There are three variables that can undermine the effectiveness of this therapy. First, some tumors produce larger amounts of catalase which neutralizes the oxidizing effect of hydrogen peroxide. Second, sometimes there is an insufficient number of catalysts to promote the transfer of electrons. Third, sometimes there is an insufficient amount of oxygen in the extracellular space, which is needed in order for vitamin C to produce hydrogen peroxide.

For now, scientists have not found a way to selectively block the production of catalase within tumors. However, we can definitively increase the effectiveness of this therapy by providing two supporting agents—electron transfer catalysts and tumor oxygenating agents.

Vitamin C & K3

The ability of vitamin C to generate hydrogen peroxide in tumors hinges on the presence of catalysts that can transfer electrons from the vitamin C to oxygen molecules, generating an unstable compound superoxide which rapidly converts to the hydrogen peroxide that possesses cancer-killing properties. One well-known catalyst with this capability is menadione, also known as vitamin K3.[14] There is substantial research in both rodent and human studies that demonstrates that supplementing intravenous vitamin C therapy with injectible vitamin K3 increases the effectiveness of the therapy on cancer cells.

Researchers at the Catholic University of Louvain, Belgium, have played a pioneering role in demonstrating the potential of the vitamin C/vitamin K3 combination in cancer treatment. In particular, they have shown that the combined administration of these agents can retard cancer growth and metastasis in tumor-bearing rodents.[14-16] They also report that this therapy is well tolerated, without any evident damage to healthy tissues.

They also demonstrate that the vitamin C/vitamin K3 combination can interact synergistically with certain cytotoxic chemotherapy drugs in killing cancer cells. This is logical since, as I mentioned before, some chemotherapy drugs work by increasing the levels of oxidative stress within cancer cells. Indeed, there are reports that vitamin K3 alone can increase the cytotoxicity of certain chemotherapy agents, presumably because, in sufficiently high concentrations, vitamin K3 helps generate oxidant stress by transferring electrons from intracellular molecules to oxygen.[17, 18]

At the Oasis of Hope we inject vitamin K3 just prior to the vitamin C infusions, with the hope and expectation that the vitamin C/vitamin K3 combination will markedly increase the production of hydrogen peroxide within tumors, enabling a more substantial cell kill in those cancers that produce sufficiently small amounts of catalase. While vitamin K3 is an excellent electron transfer catalyst, the effectiveness of intravenous vitamin C therapy can still be crippled if the oxygen levels within the tumor are poor! Since many common tumors create a hypoxic, or oxygen poor, environment, it is necessary to introduce agents that can efficiently oxygenate those tumors.

Lack of Oxygen in Tumors

In 1992, the National Cancer Institute sponsored a conference which emphasized the importance of developing methods to overcome tumor hypoxia. Remember that many tumors create an oxygen-poor environment, making them harder to kill because the anti-tumor therapies depend on the presence of oxygen to create unbearable levels of oxidative stress. In fact, not only is intravenous vitamin C therapy oxygen dependent, but so are chemotherapy and radiation therapy.

So, tumor hypoxia has been the stone in the oncologist's shoe for a long time. The NCI called for a solution to tumor hypoxia in 1992 and it took over a decade for an answer to surface. Researchers at the Canary Islands Institute for Cancer Research developed an effective tumor oxygenating technique. In 2004, Dr. Bernardino Clavo and his cohorts reported in an article titled "Ozone Therapy for Tumor Oxygenation" that ozone therapy increases oxygenation in the most poorly-oxygen tumor tissues.[19]

Oxygenating Tumors

He recruited eighteen cancer patients and used special needle probes to measure the oxygen content of their tumors before and after three sessions of ozone autohemotherapy (O3-AHT). In this procedure, the doctor draws 200 ml of the patient's blood, which is ozonized and re-infused into the patient. Dr. Clavo established that there were fewer hypoxic tumor regions following O3-AHT[19] because it makes blood less viscous, red blood cells more flexible, and more prone to surrender oxygen.[20] He also found that the therapy promotes vasodilation, a widening of the blood vessels caused by the release of nitric oxide from the endothelial lining of small arteries. The net result of all of these therapeutic effects is a significant increase in the delivery of oxygen to the tumor site.[19]

This is one method we use at Oasis of Hope to oxygenate tumors in preparation for anti-tumor therapy. The O3-AHT is an important preparatory step for intravenous vitamin C therapy, chemotherapy, and radiation therapy. In addition to oxygenating tumors, O3-AHT also present a wide range of immune-stimulating effects that greatly benefit the overall health of the patient.

This procedure is typically repeated several times weekly. It is important to stress that Oasis of Hope employs an O3-AHT protocol that has been widely used in Europe with an excellent safety record. The safety of this strategy reflects the fact that no ozone is directly infused into the body. Ozone is very unstable, so we make sure it is completely dissipated in the ozone-treated blood before the blood is returned to the body. Thus, the body is exposed to the positive by-products of ozone oxidation rather than the ozone itself. The exposure of blood to ozone in clinically appropriate amounts does not damage the cell membranes of red blood cells, or compromise the growth and development of white blood cells. In fact, no evident side effects are noted in patients receiving O3-AHT.

A second tumor oxygenating method we use at the Oasis of Hope is a novel product called Perftec. In 2005, this product was approved by the Mexican FDA as a blood substitute because of its incredible capacity to carry oxygen.[21] I became aware of this product in 1998 and started the registration process in Mexico. There is a great need for Perftec in Mexico, because blood donations are so low that only half of the blood needed by emergency rooms is collected every year. This leaves millions of patients who need blood stranded. The second reason I spent nearly seven years working to register Perftec in Mexico was to further increase the effectiveness of the anti-tumor treatments my cancer patient's receive.

Perftec is an incredibly small oxygen carrying particle. It is 100 times smaller in diameter than a red blood cell. This means it can carry oxygen through the smallest of vessels. Perftec has proven to increase oxygen levels in tumors like this and render oxygen-dependent therapies much more effective.

In some patients with stubborn and resilient tumors that present an immediate life-threatening danger, we recommend chemotherapy. Now, we can dramatically multiply the oxidizing effect of chemotherapy by coupling that treatment with intravenous vitamin C and vitamin K3, O3-AHT, and Perftec.[22-28] This Oasis of Hope strategy has been designed to leverage the complementary interactions of these therapies so that the destruction of cancer cells is maximized without an increase in the toxic risk to healthy tissues.

We thoroughly discuss every aspect of our treatment protocols with each and every patient. While we may recommend complementary chemotherapy when it presents a benefit, ultimately each patient decides what to include or exclude in regard to their own cancer treatment. Our preliminary results are showing us that this "oxidizing" strategy is working. Our patients are experiencing tumor reduction, increased longevity, and improved quality of life. I know that give-and-take is the central principle of diplomacy, but when cancer is concerned I say "give one and take ten." May cancer rust in peace! The hope provided by therapies that effectively and efficiently oxygenate tumors is another important piece of the integrative regulatory therapy offered at the Oasis of Hope.

Ricky Deniz

For an effective oxidative stress therapy, avoiding free radical runaway production is paramount; even when no chemotherapy is used. This is achieved by providing extrinsic electrons through our Redox Regulatory Therapy. High dose Vitamin C is an effective oxidative stress therapy. Rickie's extremely aggressive stomach cancer responded impressively to an all-natural therapy. Here is his testimony…

- Dr. Contreras

"It's really amazing. I had five tumors in my liver before I came to the Oasis of Hope. In my last CAT Scan, the doctors told me that I only had one tumor left that was active. When I came back the last time, the doctors said that the tumor had shrunk down to half of what it was before. The wonderful thing also is that the tissue in my liver has grown back. It's like I have a new liver. My liver is now normal and I'm praising God because I know that it is the treatments. I know that the Lord sent me to Oasis of Hope and He's used the knowledge of the doctors to get me through this disease. I'm truly thankful.

When I first stepped into the Oasis of Hope, it felt different. It did not feel like a hospital. I had been in many hospitals before. It felt like I was coming home. I just didn't know what to expect. When the staff welcomes you, they are just not welcoming you, they are welcoming you and your family. That's made me feel very comfortable. Right away you have somebody to talk to.

When I first started the treatment, I was hesitant about the effectiveness of the treatment. I prayed that it would work. However, if there is one thing you learn when you get here is that this is a place of real hope. The Oasis of Hope is not just a hospital, it's a spiritual retreat where they treat your body, mind, and spirit. And in order to heal your body, many times your spirit or your mind needs to be healed also. This is a very special place because the Spirit of God dwells here and every single person in this hospital that I've ever run into, all the staff and the doctors have been fantastic. They have been kind and compassionate. The doctors have been very knowledgeable and very supportive. A man here told me once, 'A person won't let you help them unless they know you care.' At the Oasis of Hope, you know they care. I think that has made the biggest difference in my experience at the Oasis of Hope. I just want to say thank you. I feel blessed that I went to Oasis of Hope and got a chance to meet everyone."

Ricky Deniz
Hawaii, USA

8

Providing resources to the body, mind, and spirit boosts the immune system.

Internal Security Team

Cats amaze me. They really do. Did you know that a cat has 244 bones and over 500 muscles? [1] Did you know that a cat has five more vertebrae in its spine than a human does? Did you know that a falling cat will always prepare for landing in a precise order? First, the cat will rotate its head. Then, the cat will twist its spine and align the rear legs. Finally, the cat will arch

Immune Stimulation

its back to better absorb the impact of the fall. What an amazing animal!

Recently, a friend of mine witnessed this ability in action. His family owns a large Mackerel Tabby. Okay, large is probably an understatement. The cat is fifteen pounds of solid muscle. They hitch a saddle to it on the weekends and charge the neighborhood kids a dollar for a ride…not really…but the cat is an absolute beast.

Anyway, this cat gave my friend quite a scare recently. He was working on the computer in the office niche built into the landing at the top of the stairs. The cat, in an effort to get some attention, leapt up onto the half-wall overlooking the stairs. In the blink of an eye, the cat's rear legs slipped over the edge and the cat was hanging on for dear life. Before my friend could grab a paw, the cat was upside down and falling twenty feet. Sure enough, this beast of a feline deftly performed the reflexive series of corrective maneuvers and landed on the hardwood floor as light as a feather. Then, it walked away like nothing happened. Incredible!

Natural Defenses

Similarly, the human body possesses an amazing ability to protect itself from all kinds of harm. Our bodies are constantly engaged in the action of neutralizing danger outside and inside. We call this the immune system.[2] The immune system is a group of mechanisms within the body that protects against disease by identifying and killing pathogens, or germs, and mutated cells, or tumors. Most importantly, the immune system can distinguish the difference between dangerous elements and healthy cells.

At Oasis of Hope we include a number of agents that can aid the immune system's ability to attack cancer by optimizing the function of natural killer cells and cytotoxic T-cells. Natural killer cells have the potential to kill a broad range of cancer cells, whereas cytotoxic T-cells target cancer cells that express specific proteins not produced by healthy tissues. Although immune cells are rarely capable of destroying large tumors, they have good potential for killing the small nests of tumor cells that give rise to new metastases or that can cause a recurrence of cancer following a remission. Therefore, boosting the activity of natural killer cells and cytotoxic T-cells is the first piece of the Oasis of Hope immune stimulation therapy.

Melatonin

One of the most intriguing immuno-supportive agents employed by Oasis of Hope is the hormone melatonin, administered once daily before bedtime. Multiple clinical studies in Italy show that this substance tends to have a very favorable, statistically significant impact on survival in patients with advanced cancer.[3-5] There is reason to believe that the chief reason for melatonin's positive effect on survival in cancer patients is an immuno-stimulant effect that boosts the activity of natural killer cells and cytotoxic T-cells. This effect is indirect because melatonin actually acts on dendritic cells (specialized cells that function as antigen-presenting cells for T-cells), amplifying their capacity to stimulate natural killer cells and cytotoxic T-cells. Melatonin boosts the ability of dendritic cells to produce interleukin-12, which helps cancer-attacking immune cells reach maturity.[6-8]

Probiotics

Another set of important immuno-supportive agents are probiotics. These are enterically-coated capsules which introduce live healthy bacteria into the gastrointestinal tract. Enteric coating protects the capsules from stomach acid so they can pass through to the intestines. The bacteria that are chosen for this supplement include special strains of Lactobacilli and Bifidobacteria. These bacteria can stimulate the immune system because of the polysaccharides in their cell walls. These bacterial polysaccharides cause dendritic cells to encourage the growth and activation of natural killer cells and cytotoxic T-cells.[9-11] This is because the dendritic cells recognize the bacterial polysaccharides as foreign material produced by invading bacteria and they respond appropriately.

Selenium

Supplemental selenium is another immuno-supportive agent. Selenium sparks an increase in the capacity of stimulated natural killer cells and cytotoxic T-cells to express receptors for interleukin-2.[12-14] This hormone-like protein is an essential growth factor of the immune cells that attack and kill cancers. In other words, when natural killer cells and cytotoxic T-cells express receptors for interleukin-2, they grow in greater abundance.

Cimetidine

The anti-ulcer drug cimetidine is another immuno-supportive agent included in IRT protocols primarily because of firm evidence that shows it can reduce the risk of metastasis in many cancers. However, there is also evidence that cimetidine has immuno-stimulant activity for natural killer cells and cytotoxic T-cells.[15-17] These agents comprise one piece of the Oasis of Hope immune stimulation therapies.

Overcoming Immuno-suppressors

The other piece involves a number of measures that are intended to counteract the defensive measures, which tumors employ to survive. Cancers often manage to evade immune destruction by evolving mechanisms that attack immune cells, reducing their tumor-destructive capacities or even killing them. These are called "immuno-suppressive factors." By counteracting these defensive measures we can maximize the intensity of the body's immune response.

Metronomic Chemotherapy

One mechanism cancer cells use to suppress the immune system is a special cell called a T-reg cell. These are special lymphocytes that often colonize tumors and kill or disable attacking immune cells by producing immunosuppressive factors. Metronomic chemotherapy is extremely useful for controlling T-reg cells. Fortunately, T-reg cells are exquisitely sensitive to being killed by small doses of cytotoxic chemotherapy drugs. In fact, the doses are too small to harm other immune cells or cause notable side effects.[18] Remarkably, this is a case where chemotherapy can actually help boost the immune defense system!

Dicoflenac

Many tumors express an enzyme called Cox-2 that produces immunosuppressive compounds known as prostaglandins. The anti-inflammatory drug diclofenac blocks the production of prostaglandings by inhibiting the production of Cox-2. The action of diclofenac effectively blocks the tumor's defense mechanism thereby counteracting immunosuppression.

Caffeine

Adenosine is another immunosuppressive agent produced in many tumors, especially in poorly oxygenated tumor regions.[19,20] Yet, for a long time, doctors have known that the energizing effects of caffeine are evidence of caffeine's ability to block the activation of adenosine receptors in the brain. Evidently, caffeine has the same potential in tumors, offsetting the immunosuppressive activity of tumor-produced adenosine.[19] That is why, for patients who tolerate coffee easily, we recommend several cups daily.

Spirulina

The moderately oxidative environment found in many tumors is extremely toxic to natural killer cells and cytotoxic T-cells, impairing their tumor-killing capacities and even killing them. [21-23] Most of this oxidative stress is generated by a specific enzyme complex. [24,25] A key phytonutrient found in spirulina, called phycocyanobilin, functions as a potent inhibitor of this enzyme complex. This counteracts the tumor's defense mechanism by cutting at the root of oxidative stress. [26] Moreover, spirulina contains cell wall polysaccharides that stimulate immune-supportive dendritic cells.[27,28] Spirulina can act directly on some cancer cells, slowing their growth and spread. Spirulina also interferes with the angiogenic process.[25,29] So, spirulina appears to work in at least four complementary ways to slow tumor growth and support the immune system. This is why we include dietary spirulina as a part of the "At-Home" treatment program.

By bolstering the immune system, we improve the body's cat-like ability to avoid damage from infectious agents and mutated cells. In addition, by blocking the mechanisms tumors use to suppress the immune system, we can enjoy the maximum benefit of the immune system and increase the speed and strength with which it responds to the perceived threat of cancer. These therapies are yet another source of hope offered by Integrative Regulatory Therapy.

Fern Gerber

There is no disputing that a common denominator in cancer patients is that they are immune suppressed. Unfortunately, most oncologists offer little therapeutic support and virtually no advise as to how to overcome this problem. For us immune stimulation is paramount. Fern Gerber offers some words of encouragement and advice...

- Dr. Contreras

"I was diagnosed with invasive breast cancer on February 9, 2006 and that same day the surgeon asked me to make an immediate decision to undergo a lumpectomy or a mastectomy followed by chemotherapy and radiation. My first response to her was, 'I got up, got dressed and took my kids to school this morning. How did I get here?'

After asking the Lord to remove the fear that was consuming me, I decided to live by faith and also to not let cancer steal my joy. I started the Hallelujah Diet, had the lumpectomy, but refused the chemo and radiation, believing that I wouldn't survive them. I began vitamin C and supplemental therapy with my ND, but knew I needed to be somewhere where I'd receive comprehensive daily treatments and nutritional instruction. After much research, the Lord led me to Oasis of Hope where I began nutritional therapies.

At Oasis of Hope, Dr. Contreras, the whole medical team as well as the kitchen and house keeping staff worked together for my benefit. They not only treated me for the cancer, they also bolstered my immune system and through education diffused my fear of chemotherapy. In October 2008, after only two rounds of IRT, including vitamin C and chemo, the cancer has been reversed. Praise God!!

I am thankful to the team at Oasis of Hope for their dedication to research resulting in effective, non-invasive, holistic patient care, my loving, supportive husband Bernd, my family and my constant Oasis of Hope companion/best friend Yvonne."

Fern Gerber
Ontario, Canada

9

Lifestyle is far more determining than are genetics.

Healing Foods & Motion

Turn on the television. If you are like most people, you subscribe to a cable company offering several hundred channels. Use the remote to scroll through the program guide. Count the number of shows featuring weight loss or exercise programs and the number of shows featuring food or leisure activity. America, like ancient Greece, is a polytheistic culture.

Just as the citizens of that ancient empire worshipped multiple gods, who were often at odds with one another, so it is with us. We are "one nation under gods." We are a people who are clearly obsessed with being thin and fit. I mean, look at the standard body types for men and women that the entertainment industry presents. There is no question that we worship a physical ideal and often view ourselves in light of that ideal.

At the same time, we are a people equally obsessed with food and leisure activity. You cannot walk down the street of a major city without passing several fast food carts, booths, or restaurants. I can't even go to the mall without being tempted by the aroma of freshly baked Cinnabon cinnamon rolls. If that company isn't owned by Satan, I'm a monkey's uncle! As a multicultural nation, we are tempted with a vast menu of foods every day. Likewise, in the midst of our fast-paced lives, we are bombarded with images of rest and relaxation. We are obsessed with sedentary activities. As infants, we play with Leapster video games. When we become children we hold Nintendo marathons that last hours. As teens, we lounge in our bedrooms text messaging everyone we know or staring at Myspace or Facebook pages on the internet. As adults, we buy huge flat screen televisions, sofa sectionals, and leather recliners with built-in cup holders so that we can "channel surf" in comfort.

We are a polytheistic culture. Unfortunately, the god of physical fitness and the god of food and leisure are in direct conflict with each other. So, we are a nation torn between two masters. Most of us find ourselves constantly trying to keep off the pounds while we pile them on.

What Diet Is Best?

Over the years, a host of dietary recommendations have surfaced as people explored the connections between the foods we eat and our general health. There is the Atkins diet, the Bernstein diet, the Cambridge diet, the DASH diet, the Elimination diet, and the Fat Smash diet to name just a few. We could go straight through the alphabet and there would be multiple diets for every letter. Despite the claims to the contrary, many of these diets are very difficult to follow. Often they restrict so many foods that they should be renamed the "flavorless" diets.

With all of the diet and fitness information available today, just about everyone is under the illusion that they possess enough knowledge to maintain a good state of physical health. For example, lots of people think, "If I lower my intake of carbohydrates and saturated fats, then I should lose weight." Yet, when people pursue a low-carb or low-fat diet, many are shocked when they are unable to shed the pounds. This is because the actual concepts are much more complex than the simplified information presented on television shows designed to promote a specific dietary program.

Insulin Is Key

So, let me give you some accurate and expert information that will have a measurable impact on your risk for degenerative disease. Let's talk about insulin. Most people would assume that a discussion regarding insulin level in the bloodstream is only relevant to a diabetic, but nothing could be further from the truth. The presence of two hormones—insulin and the related insulin like growth factor-I (IGF-I) —directly correlates to the incidence of some cancers. In fact, controlling the levels of these hormones is one of the most important aspects in an anti-cancer regimen. They have such a significant impact in regard to cancer that is incomprehensible that any oncologist would not have a diet designed to control the production of these hormones integrated into every treatment program.

Unless you have been living in a bubble for the last twenty years, you know there is a strong connection between the foods we eat and chronic degenerative diseases. The great news is that there are also foods that rebuild a healthy body. The China Study has been of particular interest to me because it singles out the foods that are absolutely linked to an increased risk for cancer. The China Study, conducted by Cornell University, is an ongoing study that has spanned a period of over twenty years in rural China. The participants in this study ate a diet that was primarily plant-based. Guess what? The study showed that risk for most cancers correlated with the proportion of dietary calories provided by animal products.

So, what exactly are animal proteins, animal fats, processed foods, processed sugars, and white flour doing that increases the risk for cancer? A diet based largely on these staples of a "western" diet boosts our production of two important hormones: insulin and "free" insulin-like growth factor-I, or IGF-I. At the Oasis of Hope, we have carefully examined the science that links the levels of these hormones in the bloodstream to the rapid multiplication of mutated cells.[1,2] The connection is clear.

These hormones block the process of cell apoptosis. Cell apoptosis is the program within a cell that tells it when it is time to die and make way for a new healthy cell to take its place. It is also the process by which mutated cells, or cancers, are eliminated. Apoptosis is the wonderful and natural process God designed to help the body protect itself from cancer. But, insulin and IGF-I block apoptosis in cancerous cells. Needless to say, this allows cancer to gain a foothold within the body. So, how can diet increase or decrease the body's production of these two hormones?

Studies have determined that dietary factors in America and other westernized nations are primarily responsible for the high levels of these two hormones. Let me explain. We tend to consume diets high in saturated fats. We also tend to carry extra weight around the abdominal area because we eat larger meals than those who live in more deprived countries. We also engage in a more sedentary lifestyle. All of these factors increase insulin production, which stimulates the production of free IGF-I.

Let's revisit the China Study. People in rural China eat a quasi-vegan diet. This diet is almost purely vegetarian coupled with an extremely limited amount of meat and dairy products. This type of diet causes the liver to decrease the production of IGF-I, and increase the production of a protein that blocks the production of free IGF-I.[3, 4] So, what impact does this information have on the treatment of cancer? Let me piece it together.

Foods that increase the levels of insulin and free IGF-I in the bloodstream will ultimately stimulate cancer's progress. Insulin and free IGF-I even are involved in the defense mechanism cancer uses to protect itself against the toxic effects of chemotherapy.[5] Conversely, a diet that keeps the levels of insulin and IFG-I low will ultimately inhibit the progression of cancer. It really is that simple.

There is an excellent study conducted by Dr. James Barnard at UCLA that demonstrated that the progression of prostate cancer was significantly stunted by reducing the levels of insulin and IGF-I in the blood through a quasi-vegan diet coupled with an exercise regimen. This was known as the Pritikin diet-exercise program.[6, 7] Dr. Barnard's study is complemented by the China Study because people living in rural China do not keep a sedentary lifestyle but exercise regularly in the course of normal day-to-day activity. Dr. Barnard's study clearly showed the combined impact of a quasi-vegan diet supplemented by regular aerobic activity. This should come as a surprise to no one because doctors have mentioned diet and exercise in the same breath since they began considering the total health of the human body.

Exercise

The impact of exercise in regard to cancer treatment was powerfully illustrated in recent studies of women with breast cancer. Because breast cancers are very sensitive to insulin activity, women who have high levels of insulin have a far poorer prognosis than those with low levels of insulin.[8, 9] Other studies also demonstrated that daily aerobic exercise, like a brisk half-hour walk every day, improves insulin sensitivity. The effect was a substantial reduction in the risk of breast and colorectal cancer mortality of 50% or more.[10-12]

Studies also show that regular aerobic exercise, prior to and during cytotoxic treatment like chemotherapy, has a favorable impact on the function of the body's immune system. In addition, the exercise tends to counteract the fatigue that is often associated with such therapies, thus having another favorable effect on a patient's quality of life.[13, 14] Again, in light of such evidence, it would be foolish to disregard the impact that regular aerobic exercise has on the total health of the body and the role it plays in the prevention and management of disease.

Therefore, at Oasis of Hope, our IRT program encourages patients to make lifestyle changes in regard to diet and exercise that will reduce the levels of insulin and free IGF-I. The ideal diet is primarily plant-based. Only 15% of the calories in a person's diet should come from fats. In addition, because carbohydrates with a high-glycemic index can boost insulin levels, the diet should provide carbohydrates from sources that are low in glycemic index. Even carrot juice has quite a bit of natural sugar. Instead, we recommend green vegetable juices.

What To Eat

Ideally, it is desirable for patients to adopt a vegan, or wholly plant-based diet, with the one exception of fish oil capsules. The omega-3 fatty acids in fish oil present numerous benefits and the fish oil capsules do not increase insulin levels. A vegan diet is low-fat and moderate in protein. The vegan diet incorporates whole-food carbohydrate sources that are low on the glycemic index, such as pastas, whole fruits, and whole-grain products like sprouted wheat breads instead of wheat-flour breads.

While this diet is ideal, it is difficult for some people to follow because it often represents a drastic change. Patients that need a gradual change can derive a modest benefit by adopting a "Mediterranean" diet. This diet discourages consumption of red meat and fatty dairy products, allows moderate amounts of lean white meat or fish, and encourages the consumption of large amounts of fruits, vegetables, beans, and whole grains. While this diet is not as effective as a vegan diet, it is a vast improvement over the diets favored by most Americans.

In addition to these dietary changes, there are a host of foods that offer a range of benefits to cancer patients. For example, did you know that consuming a moderate amount of alcohol each day has a favorable influence on free IGF-I levels and can increase life expectancy?[15-18] Here is where I deviate a bit from the science. Personally, I don't even like the smell of wine or beer. So, I totally abstain. I also believe that abstinence lowers the risk of developing alcoholism. But, if you do drink wine or beer, the science suggests it will help hold the levels of insulin and free IGF-I in check. So, there doesn't seem to be any good reason why cancer patients should abstain from alcohol if consumption stays in a healthful range. For men, that means no more than three drinks a day and for women no more than two drinks a day.

Moreover, certain vegetables like cabbage, broccoli, cauliflower, kale, onions, and garlic contain compounds that cause the body's cells to produce higher levels of antioxidants as well as enzymes which detoxify the body.[19, 20] Consuming these foods can increase the ability of healthy tissues to cope with chemotherapeutic drugs and radiotherapy, so, they may be very important to patients undergoing treatment. They may also present post-treatment benefits by helping to block the development of additional cancers. They certainly don't hurt the body at all. So, when you come to Oasis of Hope, be prepared to consume plenty of these foods because they help the body to heal. It is important for anyone managing chronic illness to view dietary changes in a positive light. Giving up "comfort foods" is a small price to pay in order to halt the growth and spread of cancer.

Another food with particular promise for cancer patients is spirulina. Spirulina is a food supplement produced primarily from two species of blue-green algae. Research shows that spirulina contains a phytonutrient that blocks a signal pathway that makes cancer cells more aggressive and that protects them from programmed cell death.[21-23] In addition, spirulina contains polysaccharides that boost the ability of the natural killer cells of the immune system to block metastasis.[24] Some of this information may be a bit technical but the point is that spirulina is a must for any anti-cancer diet.

Spirulina is available in a powder and can be easily blended into smoothies made with juice, soymilk, bananas, or other whole fruits. Two heaping tablespoons of spirulina daily is an easy addition to a vegan or Mediterranean diet. There are many other foods that offer preventative antioxidant benefits. When you come to Oasis of Hope, we will be sure to educate you further in regard to the full range of foods that can offer serious benefit to your total health. If you ask, we will gladly share our recipes and teach you how to prepare some of wonderful healthy dishes.

Let me restate that all dietary changes should be complemented by regular aerobic exercise. This means exercise where the patient supports his or her own weight and moves non-stop for roughly thirty minutes. Taking a brisk walk or using exercise equipment like stair-climbers, elliptical gliders, and treadmills, will provide aerobic benefits. There is a wealth of research that details the numerous benefits of regular aerobic activity. Google the benefits of aerobic exercise and you will generate a list of web hits that would take a year to read. There is a gym near our treatment center and we provide free passes to our patients and companions to encourage regular exercise. We are also located three blocks from the beach so many of our patients take advantage of this and go for walks, enjoying the view of the Coronado Islands and the Pacific Ocean.

Remember, the goal of the Oasis of Hope approach to the treatment of cancer is to intervene simultaneously in as many ways as feasible to promote the death of cancer cells and block the spread of cancer cells. This is the most effective way to control cancers and keep them from becoming aggressive. How foolish would we be not to acknowledge the impact of diet and exercise in that effort? There is so much evidence now that clearly suggests a range of cancer-specific benefits that can be derived from healthy diet and regular aerobic activity.

While it is true that our doctors and nurses have earned many accolades, it would be wrong not to acknowledge the kitchen staff at Oasis of Hope. Food Network introduces us to many famous chefs, but many of them rely on the three Bs: butter, butter and butter. Our team doesn't have access to heavy butters, fatty meats, and many of the ingredients that are staples in the kitchens of celebrity chefs. Our cooks have access to vegetables, legumes, healthy oils, natural spices, and a few other things. Yet, they take these simple ingredients and present them in some very inviting ways. They are artists, if not magicians, and I invite you to take a look at some of their culinary masterpieces on our website www.oasisofhope.com.

In addition, our cooks perceive themselves to be members of the medical team at Oasis of Hope. They have servants' hearts and often go out of their way to prepare special dishes to address the needs and requests of patients.

Food & Fellowship

Once a week, our hospital staff prepares a cultural food festival where they transform the dinning commons into a regional restaurant. We have had festivals celebrating the food and culture of Mexico, Germany, Japan, China, Italy, and many other countries. This week, we turned the dining hall into a slice of Spain. I am looking forward to eating some "tapas." Not only is the food delicious, but the recipes are accessible and easy to follow. These are foods you can make for yourself. Our staff is committed to providing our patients with the information they need to maintain these dietary changes at home.

The menu at Oasis of Hope embraces all the concepts presented in this chapter. The foods we prepare help the body heal. Mealtime is also one of the most enjoyable times at the hospital. The tables are round which creates a natural opportunity to form friendships with other patients. I believe that it is around the table where some really important support communities are formed. When people eat healthy food prepared lovingly in an environment that encourages conversation and laughter, good things are bound to happen. This is another unique aspect of Oasis of Hope. When you are a patient or companion at our hospital, you become part of a community, part of a family. Together, we share a common goal and we partner with you for life.

Diet and exercise are clear sources of hope offered by the solid IRT program at our hospital, but the community formed at the table hints at another important part of our program—an emotional support network. Let's look at the impact of a solid support network in the next chapter.

黒田　幸子　　　　　　　　　　●

Even when a remission is achieved, many people live with the fear that cancer will come back. Statistically, it is true in many cases. It's important for us to partner with patients for life and support them whether the outcome is positive or negative. This builds hope because a patient knows that no matter what, they are not alone. I think you will see what I mean when you read this testimony...

- Dr. Contreras

"I was a patient with breast cancer that relapsed every year before I went to Oasis of Hope. Every time it came out of remission, I would have to undergo surgery, more radiotherapy, and anticancer drug treatments. I was loosing hope that I would live through this and I was experiencing painful days. Moreover, whenever I would have any pain or illness, I would immediately think that it was because of another relapse. It was so hard for me. Then, a special person took me to the Oasis of Hope Hosptial. I was surprised because it did not feel like a typical hospital. The doctors and the nurses were very cheerful, and even the patients with severe conditions have hope. I thought to myself, 'This is the hospital which really has the Hope.' I began my treatment. Unlike in previous treatments where the tumor was the thing that got any attention, they attended the needs of the entire body. My illness was painting a dark picture for the future before; but, there is a bright future for my life now. I'm living my life and improving the immunity of my entire body now. I appreciate the Oasis of Hope Hospital. I really respect the doctor who told me not to give up."

黒田　幸子
Japan

115

Overcoming cancer is so much more involved than just getting hooked up to treatment. The overall condition of a patient's body is key. Initially, we concentrate on helping a person's organs and immune system function properly. This always helps diminish side effects and promotes a successful outcome. This is what can happen when integrative therapies are used...

- Dr. Contreras

"I was a lung cancer patient. In places, the tumor was really bad and the treatment didn't go well. The doctor told me that it was impossible to do a surgery. This made me think that I was going to loose my life. The tumor grew little by little, and I couldn't use anticancer drugs because of the side effects. At that time, I found the Oasis of Hope Hospital. They helped detoxify my body and improve my immune function. I really felt power coming from my body everyday because of those treatments. The doctor's strength became my power. The tumor died imperceptibly away and I'm enjoying life now everyday. I learned not only about the treatment, but also about the importance of proper nourishment. I'm so much better than before I got cancer. I really appreciate the Oasis of Hope Hospital."

Japan

10

The power of hope is priceless in times of uncertainty.

A Healthy Perspective

It was 1978 and my eyes were glued to the television screen as the live audience chanted, "That's incredible!" One of the show's hosts, I think it was John Davidson, introduced a 6' 3" man from India who was going to squeeze himself into a 2' x 2' x 2' glass box. It did not seem possible. Yet, this Guru worked to slow his heart rate and his breathing. He became so relaxed that

he was able to contort himself into the box without suffocating. I was totally dumbstruck. Thirty years later, major universities continue to study the power of the mind.

Mind Over Cancer

The terminology used by researchers today is very impressive. Two of the most current areas of study are psychoneuroimmunology and psychoneuroimaging. A number of scientists in these fields claim that cancer doesn't have anything to do with the integrity of the immune system. They say that when you look at the immune system, there is nothing missing. It is complete, yet cancer patients are immuno-depressed. They propose that the suppression of the immune system has to do with the mind. The truth of this psychoneuroimmunological claim has been supported by a number of clinical trials. In one study, the pineal gland was removed from rats. This gland is responsible for producing melatonin and, when it is removed, no melatonin is produced. Without melatonin, an anti-cancer element called interleukin-2 was not produced. Thus, cancer occurred in the rats. There is a direct connection between the mind and cancer because immuno-suppression is a direct result of emotional thought.

So, two important questions to ask are, can we establish thinking that boosts the immune system and the production of anti-cancer agents and can we restore pyschoneuroimmunological biochemistry and psychoneuroendocrine balance? I told you the terminology was impressive! You better take a deep breath if you want to try and repeat those questions to anyone. In short, the answer is "yes."

One recent study administered melatonin and interleukin-2 to patients with end-stage cancers to compensate for the patients' suppressed immune systems. The end result was either the slowed growth of the cancer or a reduction in the size of the cancer. Back in the 1960s, my father was not trying to compensate for the suppressed immune systems of his patients by administering medications. Instead, he recognized the power of the brain and helped patients naturally increase the production of melatonin and interleukin-2 by fostering healthy thinking. Once again, Dr. Ernesto Contreras, Sr. was way ahead of his time. He absolutely knew that if a patient could harness the power of the brain, the probability that the patient could then effectively manage their cancer would increase exponentially. Recognizing the power of the brain was the key to him.

Since the technology boom of the 1980's and 1990's, people have made comparisons between the brain and a computer. For example, some estimate that the brain's storage capacity is somewhere in the range of 1 to 1,000 terabytes. A single terabyte is equal to 1,000 gigabytes. The reality is that all of those comparisons fail at a very basic level. The brain uses a neural net and is far more sophisticated than even the most powerful of computers. A computer hard drive stores things in their original and unchanged state, but this is not true of the brain.

The Power of Perspective

The brain interprets a new experience in relation to past experiences, in relation to current emotional state, in relation to cultural identity, in relation to spiritual values, and even in relation to current physical condition. Neural networks build bridges between things and the bridges that are built shape our perspective of those things. No doubt you have heard it said that a singular event witnessed by four different people will yield four distinctly different retellings of the event. The question is can we build new connections between things that change our perspective?

The influential Russian leader Vladimir Lenin stated that the death of one was a tragedy but that the death of a million was just a statistic. What a testimony that is to the power of perspective! The idea that the death of a single loved one would feel tragic, but that the death of 25 million would only register in the brain as a statistic is frightening. Sometimes we experience something so devastating that it seems the event is etched into our consciousness forever. While what happened cannot change, the meaning of the event can! Psychologists call this a reframing.

Let me give you an example of a reframing experience. Once in our hospital, on the first Worldwide Cancer Prayer Day, a patient told me that he didn't need to be healed. He said that he had a firm faith but that he had been so blessed that he didn't require God to heal him. The people in the room were confused, but the patient insisted that cancer had not been a tragedy for him. In fact, a number of blessings had come as a result. Then, he told his story.

Six months earlier, he had sat in a medical office and listened to the word "terminal." He responded first with intense fear and later with deep anger. "I'm 57 years old," he thought, "How could God do this to me?" The doctors told him that it would require heavy chemotherapy to simply prolong his life for a year. In his desperation, he decided to tie up some loose ends. So, he called his three sons to tell them the bad news. They were very supportive and worked hard to spend quite a bit of time with him.

All of his sons' marriages were failing and they were separated from their wives. But because this man was a kind father-in-law, the ex-wives began to visit him as well. There followed some awkward encounters between the couples. After a few months, he discovered that he felt much better emotionally even though treatment was not keeping the cancer from advancing. "I got a healing miracle in a more important area...my family." The awkward encounters resulted in two restored marriages. "Two back together, one more to go," he said, "If I get healed today, maybe my other son won't get back with his wife!"

His story reminds me of the story of the blind man in the Bible. In the time of Christ, people often believed that physical infirmity was an outward sign of sin in a person's life. So, the religious teachers asked Jesus whose sin was to blame for the man's blindness, his or his parents. Jesus saw things differently and told them that the man's blindness was not the result of anyone's sin. He told them that the man's blindness had a purpose and that God was going to use the infirmity to reveal his power, glory, and mercy through a healing miracle so people would believe in Him.

Forty-five years ago my father decided to offer both cancer patients and the oncologists who treat them a "reframingexperience." He strongly believed that a shift in perspective could change the lives of cancer patients and their oncologists for the better. This new perspective could be shaped with the help of two foundational concepts. By working diligently to build as many connections between personal experience and these ideas he believed patients could alter their perspective of the disease. Here are the two foundational concepts.

Don't Shoulder The Burden Alone

The first is that there are experts in the field whose job it is to shoulder the burden of treating the disease. There are countless men and women working in research laboratories, universities, and hospitals around the world. These people have dedicated their lives to studying how cancer works and how both natural and chemical measures impact the disease. The experts are constantly working to develop increasingly more effective therapies. Every cancer patient and oncologist needs to remember the size and power of that collective effort.

This does not mean that we are passive participants. What it does mean is that even though cancer feels personal, no patient or oncologist should feel they have to shoulder the burden alone. There is hope in the collective effort. There is strength in numbers. We are not alone. Not now. Not ever. We recognize the power of perspective and work to help patients and doctors alike embrace the hope of the collective effort and relinquish the emotional burden and isolation that cancer can encourage.

Victory Is More Than A Cure

The second concept is even more revolutionary. Patients and oncologists must dispense with the lie that victory is defined by a cure. The patient does not need to be cured of cancer to have victory over it. Oncologists do not have to cure cancer to have victory over it. Instead, we must learn to manage the disease, as one would a chronic illness, and be good stewards of all of the resources available to us. We know so much now about how the disease functions that control is a far more viable goal than a cure ever will be.

We must reject the societal definition of victory, where the enemy is totally eliminated. What an antiquated perspective! As I have mentioned earlier, I would rather a patient enjoy meaningful successes than meaningless successes. Many patients "fail" to eliminate their cancer but successfully manage the illness and live much longer; many times, decades longer than they were expected to live. In addition, they successfully enjoy a high quality of life during the years that they manage the disease. Now that is a true reframing experience.

Develop A Support Network

Not only must people work to reframe their perspective of cancer, but they must seek to develop a strong support network that sustains them with words and acts of encouragement. I remember a schoolmate and friend that had a haemangioma that covered more than half his face. It was a horribly thick, blue, and purple mole that deformed the right side of his forehead, eyelid, ear, nose, and lips. He looked like a monster from a horror movie. The sight of him caused a mixture of disgust, discomfort, and sorrow in most people.

Yet, my friend had no need for a mask. He never felt compelled to hide his deformity. The thinly disguised reactions of the people around him didn't bother him. He was a happy and outgoing teenager. I admired him for that. Once, he confided in me that he was vaguely aware of the repulsive quality of his appearance, but that ever since he could remember, his father had told him that God had given him his distinctive looks because he was very special. Those words had taken root in his heart and they had made all the difference.

My friend's father was not a psychologist. In fact, he hardly had any education at all, but earned his living working in a flower shop. However, he understood the life-changing and perspective-shaping power of words. Now my friend is a very able and successful emergency medical technician and works for one of the most important ambulance services in all of Mexico. We recognize the impact of words on the emotional strength of patients, and teach them how to absorb words selectively.

This may be one of the hardest aspects of managing an illness. Learning how to sift through the various words of support and advice, all the while determining what will truly strengthen the emotions and support a proper perspective, is not easy. This is partly because people speak without really thinking about and truly understanding the meaning and impact of what they are saying.

One of the best experiences I ever had was a counseling internship at a bereavement center. It taught me a lot about the power of words.

I learned that most people know little about the grieving process and next to nothing at all about supporting a person who has suffered a loss. In the support group I was facilitating, there were men whose wives died from cancer or emphysema. There were women whose husbands died suddenly from heart attack or stroke. There were people who had lost parents to murder, siblings to suicide, and children to drug overdose. Frequently, they would discuss the ignorant and hurtful words some well-meaning person shared with them.

"Well, he was very old. So, it was to be expected."

"Three months have gone by, aren't you over it yet?"

"Just get on with your life!"

"Don't cry. You have to be strong."

"How are you doing?"

As the group shared, they would begin in tears, continue in anger, and end in laughter. I was amazed at how much time we spent laughing at one preposterous comment after another. I asked a number of our patients at Oasis of Hope if they had to endure insensitive comments from time to time. A patient told me, "Once a person said to me, 'I hope you don't feel as bad as you look!'" It is hard to believe that someone would say such a thing, but I have heard much worse. This is what happens when people disengage the brain from the mouth.

Ignorance is not an excuse but it does help explain why people make such comments. The people who say things which are not helpful don't have a clue what they are talking about because they don't share the patient's unique experience. How could anyone know what to say when they have not experienced exactly what the patient is experiencing? Every person's experience is uniquely their own and it requires a lot of listening to learn exactly what that person wants and needs to hear from those who they turn to for support.

Anxiety is another reason why people make such comments. Well-intentioned people feel anxious because they want to say the right thing but have no idea what that right thing is. Their anxiety is amplified by silence, because they fear that their silence will be interpreted as a sign that they don't care. So, in desperation, they search for something to say and often wind up blurting out something that does not achieve the effect they desired. They often realize they said the wrong thing the second after they speak it. This, in turn, causes more anxiety.

People who are managing cancer are going to experience these encounters frequently, perhaps even on a daily basis. The result is that many are tempted to isolate themselves from others and any possible emotional support network. I cannot emphasize enough what a huge error in judgment that is. A well-functioning social support network is vital to patient recovery. We teach patients how to construct, develop, and maintain a healthy social support network. Here are seven strategies to consider.

Ways To Filter, Focus & Benefit

First, people must learn to collect valuables. They must pay close attention to the things people say to them because sooner or later someone is going to say something that makes them feel really good. Someone will listen carefully, think clearly, and speak thoughtfully. Their words will be a light in darkness. Patients who are learning to manage an illness must learn to recognize words that have value and learn to collect them in their heart. There are numerous collection strategies. One is to write down what was said in order to revisit it again and again.

Second, people must learn to eliminate garbage. Again, they must pay close attention to the things people say to them because people will say things that do not make them feel good. It is important for patients to recognize the garbage words for two reasons. One, it helps further define the types of comments that do feel good. Two, it makes it easier to filter out similar comments in the future. Patients who become skilled in this regard have a much easier time letting harmful comments roll off them like water off a duck's back.

Third, people must learn to vent. Sometimes a comment is so insensitive that it instantly penetrates the heart. Sometimes the heart reaches a saturation point, like a sponge that can't soak up another drop of water. When this happens it is important for patients to find healthy ways to blow off steam. There are lots of ways to vent. Some patients cry with a close friend, some talk with a support group, some hit baseballs in a batting cage. What matters is that they recognize and satisfy the need to release pent up emotions in a way that truly makes them feel better.

Fourth, people must learn to politely end conversations. It never helps to get bent out of shape or to be nasty with people. The amount of negative energy it requires does more harm than good. However, when patients find themselves in a conversation that is headed in a very familiar and negative direction, it is important to have a set of polite statements that will quickly and effectively end a conversation. They should be short and end on a positive note. Here are a few examples:

"I don't have anything to share at this moment but thank you for your interest and your prayers."

"I'm hanging in there. Your prayers are much appreciated. I'll see you soon. Thanks again."

"Thanks for the advice/concern/support. I'm going now to get some rest. Thank you again."

Fifth, people must learn to select members of their support team. Counselors often prescribe the practical advice "if something is helpful, do more of it." Likewise, they advise "if something is harmful, do less of it." The same principle holds true in regard to people. Once patients identify people who encourage them, they should arrange to see them often. In addition, they should work hard to limit their exposure to people who do not encourage them. Carefully and intentionally selecting a social support group is an extremely important step in the recovery process.

Sixth, people must learn how to gently train their support group. As a person discovers the types of things that do or do not encourage them, they need to communicate their discoveries to their primary support group. They might say, "You know what I've learned as I manage this illness? I've learned that comments like (give a specific example), though they are made with the best of intentions, don't make me feel encouraged." Then they might add, "I have discovered that when people say things like (give a specific example) I feel incredibly encouraged."

Finally, people must learn how to forgive others. It always amazed me how Jesus asked the Father to forgive those who crucified Him because He recognized their ignorance. There is no way to escape it. People will say outrageous and hurtful things out of ignorance or anxiety. However, nursing a grudge is not an effective way to blow off steam and it will not help a person recover. Learning to forgive people for their well-intentioned ignorance or for cracking under the pressure of anxiety will help keep a person moving along a path to recovery.

In addition to reframing one's emotional perspective of cancer and building a healthy social support network, it is important to learn how to filter and focus in regard to advice. I am always amazed at how many people have the "solution" to someone else's "problem." They come in all shapes and sizes. Some are sales people. Some are know-it-alls. Some are the "I-had-the-same-problem-and-this-is-what-worked-for-me people." There is no way to listen to and incorporate all of the advice people offer. So, patients must learn to filter first.

The best way to filter advice is to conduct a bit of research. People who study literature that is relevant to their condition are better equipped to determine whether or not an individual is sharing something helpful. When people don't read up on their condition, they cannot filter out unwanted advice and the result is a tremendous amount of anxiety and confusion. Often these patients make decisions that are motivated by fear and anxiety. Getting informed makes it easy to filter and it also makes it easy to focus.

The best way to focus on expert advice is to conduct a bit of research. Everybody needs to hear the voice of reason. Doing some careful research leads patients to a number of experts. People should choose an expert to act as the voice of reason and they should honor the informed choice they made by focusing on that voice. People can gain incredible comfort by focusing their attention on the advice of a deeply committed professional. We help educate patients so they can filter and focus.

One must not only learn to reframe perspective, develop support, and filter advice, but one must learn to accept kindness. People are often overwhelmed when others say, "If you need anything, just let me know." While it is a wonderful experience, having someone offer help, it is an uncomfortable experience accepting that offer. This is not because it would be inappropriate to accept help, but rather because we are so unaccustomed to accepting the help of others. We are a culture of do-it-yourselfers. Grabbing a helping hand does not come easily to us.

Accept Help

People who are managing cancer must learn to accept kindness. They will actually be doing the person who offers to help a favor by being very specific about the type of support they need. Those who offer to help are often just as ignorant and anxious as those who offer words of support and advice. By accepting the offer quickly and indicating a specific area of need both the ignorance and the anxiety are eliminated. Here are just a few things a person could say in response to an offer of help:

"You know what? I could use some help making dinner for my family one night a week."

"Thank you so much. I could use some help vacuuming my house just one day a week."

"I appreciate your offer. I do need an occasional ride to the hospital for treatment."

"I would love your help. I need someone to go grocery shopping for me once a week."

Learning to reframe perspective, develop support, filter advice, and accept kindness are all critical components to developing a healthy emotional state while managing challenging circumstances, including cancer. The synergistic effect of a strong and healthy emotional state on the management of illness is very powerful. Doctors have long known that depression and emotional stress can severely depress the immune system and negatively affect the body's response to treatment. By developing strong emotional support we positively impact virtually every aspect of a treatment program.

I believe that good treatment programs do not narrow their focus to the treatment of the body, but embrace the necessity of treating the whole person — body, mind, and spirit. I believe that the dramatic shift the medical community is poised to make in regard to the management of cancer as a chronic illness will cause them to widen their focus in order to nurture the emotional health of the patient as well. Oasis of Hope is already committed to teaching our patients how to develop strong emotional support networks that last a lifetime.

How You See Things

I am always impressed with the emotional fortitude of the outdoorsmen who host those wilderness adventure shows. I don't know about you, but if I were stuck high up in the Rocky Mountains, or deep in the Bornean rainforest, or far out in the Mojave Desert, I would not be in a particularly upbeat mood. I'm not sure how these guys manage to find a silver lining in just about every situation, but they do. What I do know is that they are an absolute testament to the power of perspective. I want people who manage cancer to tap into that power.

Just as I find the attitude of those wilderness show hosts baffling, I believe a time is here when people who live with chronic disease, like cancer, will possess an equally baffling attitude. They will be happy and focused and energetic and able to see the silver lining in their own lives because they are surrounded by a team of experts who recognize the importance of emotional strength and who work with them and help them to reframe perspective, develop support, filter advice, and accept kindness.

The truth is that all of these strategies can be applied to whatever challenges you face in life. But if the challenge is cancer, please put these tactics to work for you. I truly admire the insight my father had when he noted that a doctor cannot merely treat a patient's body. A doctor has to be more than a drug dispenser. He must be a friend, counselor, teacher, and intercessor. He must be a healing partner for life. So, in 1963, he set up the Oasis of Hope to provide total wrap-around care that meets all of a patient's needs. We continue to help our patients regain health of body, mind, and spirit. Almost half a century later, we honor the legacy of Dr. Ernesto Contreras, Sr.. We provide laughter therapy, music therapy, art therapy, and pet therapy. We facilitate group discussions regarding community building, coping skills, and stress management. We are committed to diminishing the negative effects of stress and depression by helping patients embrace a new perspective that yields anti-cancer benefits. This is another critical part of the hope offered in our IRT program at Oasis of Hope.

In addition, we don't ignore the physiological impact of faith. We offer daily devotions, praise and worship services, and Sunday school because we recognize the importance of spiritual health as well. Let's take a closer look at this component in the next chapter.

Dr. Fred Mendoza

Today's faith increases when recounting God's work in your past. No one should ever underestimate the power of faith. I think this rings true in Dr. Mendoza's testimony...

- Daniel Kennedy

"Physically-trimmed and fit due to adhering to a healthy diet and regular exercises, being diagnosed with cancer in June 2006 was a total shock to me, my wife, our congregation and others who know me very well. With no physical pain anywhere in my body, except a small growth in my neck which I had for over a year, my primary physician's diagnosis was, 'Don't worry, your small growth in the neck is nothing to worry about.' Finally, unexpectedly, a simple biopsy from a little growth in my neck had revealed that I had non-Hodgkin's lymphoma cancer stage III!

After hearing the diagnosis, my wife left the doctor's office crying, and I just looked at the door with a big smile on my face, seemingly indicating that my cancer diagnosis did not really bother me that much. No, I didn't go through a state of denial, I didn't ask the question, 'Why me?' I didn't get angry with myself, with the Doctor, or with God. But, I bargained with God by saying, 'Lord, you had healed me when I was given three days to live, after being sick of typhoid fever for two months in the Philippines, at 16-years-old. You had also healed me of tuberculosis at age 21. If You heal me again this time, I will serve You even more than the past 48 years I have been faithfully serving You.' The good news is, the Lord healed me of cancer. How, and how quickly?

After three sessions of chemotherapy at the hospital near my home, which degraded my health and almost killed me, I decided to stop having more chemotherapy after listening to a videotape by Dr. Loraine Day, a medical doctor, who refused chemotherapy for her cancer but got well through alternative medicine. Also, a church member gave me a copy of Dr. Francisco Contreras' and Daniel Kennedy's book, *Fighting Cancer 20 Different Ways*, which convinced me to be treated at their hospital, the Oasis of Hope. I was scheduled to have four sessions of treatment for 21 days. After the first session, my stage III non-Hodgkin's lymphoma cancer was no longer detectable in my body! Even my oncologist at the hospital in Baldwin Park, California, was surprised after giving me a test that verified the report from Oasis of Hope Hospital that my cancer was already in remission. That was more than two years ago today, October 21, 2008, and I remain a very healthy 69-year-old cancer survivor. What brought about my speed and full recovery from cancer?

I'm sure the treatment at the Oasis of Hope Hospital had helped a great deal. My positive and hopeful faith in God, and the prayers of my wife, my daughter, my other relatives, and all the hosts of people who prayed for me all over the States and overseas, had miraculously brought about my healing. Yes, medicine and prayer were used by God to heal me of cancer, but I strongly believe that my healing was a direct answer to prayer more than the medical treatments I had received. To God be the glory!

To help myself beat cancer, I listened to Christian music day and night, I read my Bible daily and quoted scriptures to myself, I exercised almost everyday even when it was uncomfortable, I did not stop working. I only missed my pulpit ministry one Sunday because I was at the Oasis of Hope Hospital. I maintained a positive attitude. I shouted behind my pulpit on Sunday mornings, 'Christ can conquer cancer!' He did for me. What He has done for me, He can do for you."

Dr. Fred Mendoza,
Senior Pastor, Charisma Life Church
California, USA

11

Life and death are all about perspective.
Spiritual fortitude provides clarity to the now, the past and, more
importantly, to eternity.

True Hope, True Healing

Do you like salad? You had better…because you live in a salad bowl. Many modern historians have abandoned the "melting pot" description of America, which suggested that immigrants from all over the world came here and were fused into one culture. Now, historians describe American culture as a "salad bowl," where cultures mix  but maintain their original "flavor." Indeed, culture and tradition are important values to many Americans.

Often, part of our cultural heritage is a religious belief system. After all, the desire for religious freedom drove many early settlers to make the transatlantic crossing. We are a multicultural nation that honors a host of culturally-specific faiths. Once, I attended an Eastern Orthodox Catholic mass as part of a college course I was taking. Now, I had observed a Roman Catholic mass before, but this was completely different. It was like mass on steroids. It was an aerobic workout. Stand up. Sit down. Kneel down. Stand up. Turn right. Turn left. Do the hokey-pokey. The liturgy of an Eastern Orthodox Catholic mass is totally participatory. If it weren't for the kind souls in front of me, who I imitated the entire service, I would have been a lost cause. It was a wonderful cultural experience. Faith and spiritual health are part of the cultural landscape of America.

Faith & Healing

There are millions of pages written about the importance of maintaining physical health while managing cancer. There are millions of pages addressing the importance of cultivating emotional strength while managing cancer. However, most oncologists disregard the importance of seeking spiritual peace while managing cancer though studies indicate that patients want spiritual support and benefit from it. In the June 24, 1996 edition of *Time* magazine,[1] writer Claudia Wallis noted a growing trend in her article titled "Faith & Healing."

She found a number of scientists who were "beginning to look seriously at just what benefits patients may derive from spirituality." She said that "to their surprise, they are finding plenty of relevant data buried in the medical literature." Dr. David Larson, formerly a research psychiatrist at the National Institute of Health, uncovered over two hundred "studies that touch directly or indirectly on the role of religion," and that "offer evidence that religion is good for one's health." The findings were compelling.

The article cited a 1995 study at Dartmouth-Hitchcock Medical Center which noted "that one of the best predictors of survival among 232 heart-surgery patients was the degree to which the patients said they drew comfort and strength from religious faith." The study went on to state that the subjects who did not seek spiritual peace and comfort had a death rate three times that of the subjects who did seek spiritual peace and comfort. The article cited even more evidence of the connection between faith and healing.

A survey of over thirty years of research showed that churchgoers have lower blood pressure than non-churchgoers. Likewise, another study showed that churchgoers have half the risk of suffering from coronary-artery disease than non-churchgoers. A study of 4,000 elderly from North Carolina revealed that churchgoers were in better physical and emotional health than non-churchgoers. The question remains, however. Does spiritual peace have a physiological effect on the total health of the individual?

Dr. Herbert Benson of Harvard University has thought so for years. In his book *Timeless Healing*, Benson studied a group of patients who were managing chronic illness.[2] He noted that over a five year period those patients who drew strength from an intimate connection to God had better overall health and a more rapid rate of recovery. He even went on to say that he firmly believes that "humans are actually engineered for religious faith." This is certainly in keeping with what the Bible says about the nature and design of mankind.

Dr. Benson believes that activities designed to secure spiritual peace, such as prayer, create a physiological effect by traveling the same biochemical pathways as activities designed to create a relaxed state. These activities stimulate production of epinephrine and other hormones that positively impact blood pressure, heart rate, and respiration. Research also clearly defines the impact of these hormones on the immune system. They work to amplify the body's ability to defend itself. Yet, why not just use relaxation techniques to do this?

Dr. Benson believes that the "benefits of religious faith are even greater" than other methods. Are these scientists ready to say that churchgoers actually have God on their side? Dr. Jeffrey Levin of the University of Eastern Virginia says that "true scientists... cannot dismiss this possibility." Yet, recent surveys reveal that almost two-thirds of the physicians in the United States claim to be non-believers. This contrasts sharply with the over 80% of Americans who claim to believe in God and the over 60% who think physicians should pray with their patients.

I believe that the spiritual well-being of a person has a profound impact on their health. I believe that when treatment programs also seek to bolster a patient's spiritual well-being, it will have a positive physiological impact. However, I believe many people suffer spiritual illness that has had a profoundly negative effect on various aspects of their lives. The negative thoughts and behaviors that destroy healthy thoughts and behaviors are devastating to the immune system. Negative thoughts and behaviors are often provoked by spiritual disequilibrium.

Reflecting The Immaterial

Everything that takes place in the physical world is a reflection of what happens in the spiritual world. Genesis 1:27 tells us that God created man and woman in his image. Humanity was designed to be the mirrors that reflect the glory of God. In the same way the moon reflects the light of the sun into the darkness of the night, humanity was designed to reflect the light of the Son into the spiritual darkness of the world. We were designed to reflect God's character.

So, do we reflect the character outlined in Galatians 5:22-23, which says the character of God's Spirit is "love, joy, peace, longsuffering, gentleness, goodness, faith, meekness, and temperance." If you are filled with the fruit of the Spirit, your spirit will be balanced and healthy. But, if you find that you suffer from hatred, discord, jealousy, rage, selfishness or lack of forgiveness, you have issues to work through to restore your spiritual health.

This is why we help patients take a moment to evaluate their own lives. People need to consider the physiological impact of choosing to live in a manner that creates spiritual disequilibrium. If people were designed to reflect God's character and choose not to, they will suffer the physiological effects of spiritual imbalance.

Our body, mind, and spirit approach to medical treatment acknowledges the importance of spiritual peace and encourages patients to:

- Evaluate Their Relationship With God
- Acknowledge Areas In Need of Healing
- Seek Direction And Healing From God
- Embrace Their True Identity In Christ
- Establish A Godly Purpose For Living
- Forgive Others Including Themselves
- Adopt Godly Thoughts and Behaviors

Spiritual Peace

Why is spiritual peace such an important part of the cancer treatment program at Oasis of Hope? This is because there is a serious connectivity between the spirit, the mind, and the body. Spiritual imbalance generates negative emotion, which generates stress and distress, which depresses the immune system, which makes it easier for cancer to progress. Conversely, a healthy spiritual life generates positive emotion, which reduces stress and distress, which boosts the immune system, which fights cancer using natural killer cells and T-cells.

It may be difficult to find an oncologist working for an HMO that acknowledges the spiritual needs of his patient, but Oasis of Hope puts so much emphasis on spiritual health that some might label us a religious facility. But labeling someone "religious" today is almost an insult. Often, it implies that a person is narrow-minded and may engage in discriminatory behavior. The term didn't always imply those things. In the past, the label "religious" meant that a person possessed strong moral and ethical character.

Today, the more fashionable term is "spiritual." The term may be popular because you can say that you are spiritual and that can mean anything you want it to. Spirituality can even be commercialized. After all, even shoemakers and automakers talk about how they are green and clean. They tout their contributions to humanity. Many ecologically and socially conscious people consider themselves to be "spiritual" and companies cater to that highly-motivated market segment.

At Oasis of Hope, spirituality is not some value-added marketing ploy to leverage differentiation and positioning. It is part of the foundation of our hospital. My father often pointed out that God created humans in three parts — body, mind, and spirit. While he was in medical school in the 1930s, he became disillusioned with the unilateral focus on the disease and body of a patient. He saw a "disconnect" between the physician and the emotional and spiritual needs of the patient. He taught how true healing occurs when the body, soul, and spirit of a patient are in balance with each other. He envisioned a healing center that would minister to the physical, emotional, and spiritual needs of a patient. He saw total wrap-around care as the best means of restoring people to health. That is why he founded the Oasis of Hope in 1963. That is why we continue to build on his work now.

People from all walks of faith come to Oasis of Hope. It is common to find a mix of Christians, Muslims, Hindus, Jews, and Buddhists in our hospital. People respond to the loving environment here and the caring people who populate it. We are an unashamedly Christian facility. That fact is abundantly obvious to anyone who has read one of my books. It is equally obvious to every visitor because the walls of the hospital are covered in Scripture. However, we don't force our faith on others; we live a life of loving service to our patients. We believe this has a much more profound impact on people. In accordance with Christ's teaching, we love our patients as we love ourselves. This love and caring is an essential part of the Oasis of Hope experience and all who come here enjoy the benefit of that environment.

Spiritual health is not just a part of our anti-cancer program. It is the cornerstone of real, long-lasting health. Don't misunderstand me. Working to liberate the body of cancer is an admirable goal. Nonetheless, the results are guaranteed to be temporary. The body cannot live forever, but is destined to return from whence it came. Dust to dust, right?

Temporal Vs. Eternal Healing

In contrast, the healing of the mind and spirit is everlasting. The truth of this never hit me harder than when I heard the story of one of my patients. He was a young man, 30 years of age, who had come to the hospital with a tumor in his liver that was so large it filled his entire abdominal cavity. After two weeks of treatment, he was 100% cancer free! The only explanation I could find was that God had restored his liver like new. Our therapies are good, but not that good. It was a genuine miracle.

Three weeks after he was discharged, he stepped off a curb in downtown Los Angeles and was struck dead by a speeding bus. The news was devastating. I was seriously distressed. I realized this was because I was not sure that he had received Christ during his two-week stay at the hospital. I realized then that as amazing the physical healing he experienced was, ultimately, it was temporary. Even if he lived into his eighties, the healing would still be temporary. True healing is that which takes place in the mind and the spirit.

This brings me to another important point. If the goal of every cancer patient is to live, then doctors need to help each patient come to terms with mortality. Only then can a person live life in abundance. When people live each day in fear of death, they are slaves to fear. True hope comes from the knowledge that, through Christ, we are eternal beings and that death is not the end, but a transition. Just as the seed is transformed into a new plant, or as the caterpillar is transformed into a butterfly, so it is for our earth-bound bodies.

Let me share with you a real story to help you see death in a new light. A number of years ago, we had a patient that refused to eat or talk to anyone. Her dear husband was so desperate to help her that he would ask anybody that passed by the room to try to talk to his wife and convince her to eat. He asked me to go and try. I knelt by her wheelchair and tried to engage her in conversation. She would not talk. I got up and as I turned to walk away, her frail hand reached out and took hold of mine. In a quiet voice she asked me, "Are you the young man that was sharing a Bible story from the book of Ruth yesterday?" I told her that I was and she said, "Come by to see me tomorrow."

The next day I stopped by her room and she asked me to share the plan of salvation. I did so and asked her if she wanted to receive Jesus as her Lord and Savior. She was so weak that I had to put my ear to her lips to hear her respond, "I have been a Christian for many years." I was confused. Why had she asked me to share the plan of salvation? She saw my confusion and motioned for me to draw close again. I put my ear to her lips and I will never forget what she said next, "God's plan for us is so beautiful, isn't it? I just wanted to hear it one more time."

Two hours later she passed away. It occurred to me that the Scripture's depiction of Jesus as the waiting "bridegroom" is very accurate. That woman was the bride and I had the honor of walking her down the aisle and giving her away in those last moments. She was ready to transition to the next life and Oasis of Hope offered a spiritually charged environment that filled her with peace. It helped me understand the Scripture that says that the death of the saints is precious in the eyes of the Lord.

Remember, it is not how many days we live that matters most; it is how we spend each day that really matters. While our chief medical objective at Oasis of Hope is to extend life, we also invite people to truly engage in the life they currently have. This is much easier to do when a person develops a healthy relationship with his or her Creator.

The director of our counseling program oversees our spiritual support program, as well. This program is largely run by a volunteer ministry team called Project Oasis of Hope. The volunteers are often referred to as "Friends of Hope," or "Amigos de Esperanza." Bible studies are led by Bruce Northey and his wife Vickey. Bruce came to Oasis of Hope in 1997 with cancer and was healed here. His supervisors had a vision to start Project Oasis of Hope at the end of 1997. The volunteer organization has been in operation ever since then. In 2007, Bruce and Vickey decided to volunteer their services full-time.

Every day begins with an opportunity to attend a Bible study, a worship service, and a group discussion where people share their thoughts about their relationship with God. There are other opportunities throughout the day to attend Bible studies, worship services, and group discussions. In addition, prayer support is available to all patients at any time of the day or night. Patients can call one of the volunteers living on-site and they will come and talk to and pray with the patient in person. Following in my father's footsteps, I share a Biblical message every Sunday that I am not traveling. It is when I am sharing about the love of God that I feel most fulfilled as a doctor.

In the hospital chapel, there is a fountain with a bronze sculpture, depicting the young man born blind from the story in chapter 9 of the Gospel of John. In the story, Jesus told the crowd of on-lookers that the blindness was not the result of the boy's sin or his parents' sin. Instead, Jesus indicated that the boy had been born blind so that, on this day, God's power could be revealed in the young man's life. Then Jesus healed the young man. We want patients to know that no one "deserves" cancer. Instead, we want patients to search for the evidence of God's power at work in their lives.

Throughout this book, patients have shared their personal stories. We believe these are the types of stories readers want to hear. There are so many beautiful things that happen at Oasis of Hope. I encourage patients to look for all types of miracles. The most powerful miracles often involve the restoration of broken relationships. I have witnessed spouses fall in love all over again, I have seen brothers and sisters settle their differences, I have watched parents reach out to their estranged children for the first time, and I have been in the room when people open their hearts to a loving God. I want to cure you of cancer, but God wants to heal you forever. We may be able to help you prolong your life; God erases death (James 5:20). Jesus was clear that we will all face difficult times. True hope stems from Jesus' promise to walk difficult paths with us, and carry us when we are too weak to continue.

Bruce Northey

The first time I met Bruce, he was my patient. His name is on the first page of the Worldwide Cancer Prayer Day request book, followed by more than 25 thousand names. Now he is one of our ministry partners. What God has done in his life is simply amazing…

- Daniel Kennedy

"Hello, my name is Bruce Northey and I am a cancer victor. I would like to tell you my story. In 1995, I was diagnosed with testicular cancer. I had an operation to remove the affected testicle and was back to work in ten days. Everything happened so fast that we just went back to living our normal lives and forgot about cancer.

In 1997, after experiencing some lower back pain, I went in for a routine check-up and discovered that I had a softball size tumor that was tangled in the ureter of one of my kidneys. This reoccurrence was diagnosed as inoperable. My doctor told me I would be doing well to be alive in five years if I started treatment immediately. We decided to look for alternative treatment.

Our search led us to Oasis of Hope Hospital in Mexico. We believe very much in the power of God's word. I was given a verse to stand on before we left for Mexico. Psalm's 118:7 says, 'The Lord was with me; with them that helped me.' The power of those words unfolded right before my eyes as I began my treatment. The Oasis of Hope treatment had a wonderful effect on my life. It contributed greatly to my now being cancer free! It also encouraged me to change my lifestyle so that I can enjoy being cancer free for years to come. It was in fact such a life changing experience that my wonderful wife Vicky and I now volunteer full time at Oasis of Hope.

I truly believe there is not another healing station like this in the world."

Bruce Northey
Wisconsin, USA

12

For some, the only thing that matters is the bottom line.

A New Hope

The Oasis of Hope clinical research team developed IRT, integrating a number of therapies in order to overcome the barriers to effective cancer treatment and in order to provide an umbrella of protection to healthy cells. Our success rates show we are headed in the right direction. Not all of our patients are cured, but many enjoy an improved quality of life and increased longevity. In fact, most live much longer than previously anticipated.

There are so many wonderful things that patients experience at Oasis of Hope. I hope the testimonies included in this book help you see that many factors contribute to a person's ability to manage disease. Most patients are not just focused on a physical cure. Still, I understand and accept that the world will finally judge Oasis of Hope on our survival rates.

Results

Table I shares the preliminary results of an ongoing five-year study with our patients that have breast, lung, ovarian, or colorectal cancers. I have also included the survival rates of patients receiving "conventional treatment" in the USA. These statistics were taken from the National Cancer Institute's SEER Survival Monograph for 2007. This publication provides average cancer survival rates in major regions of the United States. When you take a look at our results, you will understand why I know we are on the right path. It is clear that, in terms of survival, Oasis of Hope patients are doing far better than those receiving the average standard of care in the U.S..

145

Table I. Survival Rates for Stage IV Cancer IRT

Type of Cancer	Oasis IRT		Conventional Treatment *	
	1-Year Survival (%)	2-Year Survival (%)	1-Year Survival (%)	2-Year Survival (%)
Breast	92	68.2	65	44
Breast**	100	88.3	65	44
Lung	76.2	41.2	20	8
Ovarian	95	76.4	62	43
Colorectal	63	42.3	43	29

*National Cancer Institute: U.S. SEER survival monograph 2007
**Patients for whom Oasis of Hope was the first treatment option

In particular, the survival rate for Oasis of Hope patients with lung cancer is strikingly better than average. We are not doing as well with colorectal cancer, but this is because colorectal cancer is typically resistant to available chemotherapies. Yet despite that fact, our results appear to be superior to conventional treatment. Note also that our results with stage IV breast cancer patients who came to Oasis of Hope soon after diagnosis are quite good, with a doubling of the two-year survival percentages relative to those who opted for conventional therapy alone.

Our patients are clearly doing better than those receiving conventional therapy. We don't claim that these patients have been "cured," in the sense that the cancer has been eliminated and won't come back, but they are certainly outliving all previous expectations. It does seem that we are making progress toward teaching patients to embrace the concept of living out their meaningful success by managing the growth and spread of disease while working to maintain a healthy quality of life. This is a far more palatable option than becoming a meaningless success enduring highly toxic treatments that successfully shrink tumors but that destroy quality of life and fail to significantly extend the life of the patient.

A big part of our success is the fact that we do not underestimate the harmful effects of chemotherapy. That is why the IRT program concentrates on protecting our patients from those harmful effects. We will always continue to work on effective alternatives that prove to prolong the lives of our patients and secure quality of life for them, as well.

You may understand why we are passionate about finding new and better ways to treat our patients. Remember, the IRT protocols are in a constant state of evolution. Barely a month goes by that we don't add some new element to the program that seems likely to improve the overall efficacy of the multi-focal treatments. So, we are optimistic. We believe we are on the right track and that our results will continue to improve over the coming years. We hope that Integrative Regulatory Therapy is firmly established as the best way to manage cancer over the long term.

Long-term Cancer Management

The concept of living with cancer over the long-term presents a conflict for many people. This is because many associate cancer with imminent death. No matter what the statistics say, reality is dictated by perceptions. Let me illustrate this truth for you. People's cancers do not come into existence the day they receive a diagnosis. Most tumors linger within the body for years before people begin to experience any recognizable symptoms. During that time, those people are not concerned about imminent death. When a malignancy is discovered, the diagnosis does not change any aspect of a person's cancer. However, the knowledge changes everything. Ignorance is bliss!

By the same token, if people receive therapy that controls cancer growth so that tumors are no longer life-threatening and quality of life is restored, then who would worry about the presence of cancer? In ever increasing numbers, patients in our hospital are "beating the odds" and experience increased longevity and improved quality of life. They are living proof that we can convert cancer from an unavoidable death sentence to a chronic but controllable disease.

But to truly overcome the threat of cancer, people must go beyond what happens to the tumors. Even when therapy is so successful that a patient is labeled "cancer free," many patients live in fear of it coming back. Why? Again, this is a battle between statistics and perspective. I believe that freedom from cancer is a matter of choice. A person can choose to be a victor over it or a victim of it. Patients who choose to see cancer as an unavoidable death sentence will always fall victim to it. Patients who choose to see cancer as a chronic but controllable disease will always have victory over it.

Choose Victory

How can you choose to be a victor? You can make this choice only when you have the emotional resources needed to challenge the traditional perception of cancer. When your being is not determined nor defined by cancer, you are a victor. A person without cancer has no assurance of a long life just as a person with cancer has no assurance of imminent death. In other words, our lives are not in our hands.

There is a story of a wealthy man in Turkey that attended to his multiple businesses from a corner office on the 7th floor of a high-rise building in downtown Ankara. He received the news that he had lost all of his assets and, in his desperation, decided to jump out of the window. His fall was initially broken by the canopy of the corner café and finally absorbed by a young man enjoying a cup of strong Turkish coffee. The young man died from the impact and the distraught and recently impoverished businessman survived with a few scratches.

Eleanor Roosevelt said "Yesterday is history, tomorrow is a mystery, and today is a gift, and that is why it is called the 'present.'" We should all live every day like it is our only day. It saddens me that so many cancer patients decide to die while they are still among the living. They die to family, they die to work, and they die to hope.

An Oasis of Hope

A person that is lost in a desert facing unlivable conditions will certainly die if he or she does not receive help from someone. An oasis in that desert means hope and life because it will provide water, food, shelter, and a shield from the elements.

In a similar way, our treatment center is an Oasis of Hope for anyone facing cancer. We strive to provide the physical, emotional, and spiritual support that restores health, hope, and faith into a patient's life. These three things are vital to abundant living, whether a person has cancer or not. Though we do not promise a cure, we make a profound commitment to wrap our care around you and offer innovative cancer therapies—some of the most avant-garde available in the world. This should give you hope. Do not let anyone rob you of hope by giving a negative prognosis. No man or woman can determine your future. If a doctor has told you or a loved one that, "Nothing more can be done," FEAR NOT. Come to a place that will shelter you in an environment of hope. You can face today with confidence because there is always something we can do for you! We want to walk with you every step of the way, using the most advanced and creative clinical strategies available. We want to give you the resources necessary to really live life, however long, to the fullest!

Batya Segal

Destroying a tumor is a very important part of therapy but anti-tumor agents are often not enough. Belief is an ingredient necessary to do away with many of the obstacles that cap your potential to beat cancer. Belief in yourself through emotional strength and belief in God through spiritual fortitude are integral ingredients to overcome any and all obstacles in life, especially cancer. Take note of how our patient Betaya Segal decided to approach her disease…

- Dr. Contreras

"The doctor looked at my mammogram, was silent for a moment and he said, 'I am sorry to tell you, but it is a malignant tumor….' At that point I couldn't hear the rest of his sentence. It was like a death verdict, but I knew that my time was not yet over. God was in all this and I did not let the fear overcome and enter me. It was most important to tell my family and explain about the diagnosis. It was vital for us to pray as a family for the next steps. The malignant tumor needed to come out either by a miracle of God or by the knife of a surgeon! In order to correct this, I realized I had, to make some radical changes in my bad eating habits and lifestyle.

Repenting of my old way of life, I sought out as much knowledge from the Lord to make the necessary changes. Asking forgiveness from those that suffered the most, particularly my family, was valuable and critical as well. For me it was a physical, spiritual, and emotional attack; therefore I reacted on those three levels. I searched for more information on the causes of cancer and what I could and should do to prevent it.

An old friend, who was very knowledgeable in alternative ways of healing through nutritional foods, spoke to me and gave me a short and a very impacting lesson. I was not sure that any of what was shared could help, but in my desperation I wanted to give it a chance. I took notes and came home to implement all that she had recommended. I cleared my kitchen cabinets and refrigerator of all the bad things that I used to eat. I became a total vegetarian and decided I would clean my body from toxins and build up my immune system. At the same time I was praying for the tumor to disappear within a certain amount of time.

I ultimately went through the surgery when I did not see the size of the tumor shrink. My surgeon recommended that I go through chemotherapy and radiation. I consulted with four specialists in Israel and came to the conclusion that it would not be the right way to go and I needed to discover another solution.

It was at that time that someone recommended Oasis of Hope, and I thought that may be the answer! I started searching their website and I communicated with them about their treatments and any testimonials from previous patients. I prayed for three things: the funds to go, the person to be with my family while I was away, and a friend to be with me at Oasis of Hope. All three were answered which was a confirmation to go.

I was introduced to a warm staff and felt right at home. The doctors were always available and patient with me; they were never too busy to answer my questions. All of the food and juices were freshly made and all organic. They taught me a new way of healthy eating and lifestyle. What I liked was the treatments that were non-invasive and their aim was to strengthen the immune system. They provided classes to educate us further about this new way of life. I feel better and have been cancer free for some years now! I am so grateful to God for all the love, help and, support I was given at Oasis of Hope."

Batya Segal
Jerusalem, Israel

References

Chapter 1

1. Roenigk, Alyssa. Liukin brings home the gold. ESPN The Magazine.Retrieved from Internet, August 31, 2008. http://sports.espn.go.com/oly/summer08/gymnastics/columns/story?id=3536410

Chapter 2

1. Discovery Channel . Man Vs. Wild. Retrieved from Internet, October 10, 2008. http://dsc.discovery.com/fansites/manvswild/manvswild.html

Chapter 3

1. Dumas, D. First Look: Microsoft Milan Surface Computer—A Table That Knows What's On It. Wired Blog Network. Retrieved from Internet, January 1, 2009. http://blog.wired.com/gadgets/2007/05/first_look_micr.html
2. Lincoln, A. The Quotations Page. Retrieved from Internet, January 3, 2009. http://www.quotationspage.com/quote/27074.html

Chapter 4

1. Pasteur, L. Quote DB. Retrieved from Internet, July 22, 2008. http://www.quotedb.com/quotes/2195
2. Leah, R. Wanderlei Silva. UFC All Access. Retrieved from Internet, September 8, 2008. http://www.youtube.com/watch?v=RWWYQGHgtEY
3. Bocci VA. Scientific and medical aspects of ozone therapy. State of the art. Arch Med Res 2006 May;37(4):425-35.
4. Bocci V. The case for oxygen-ozonetherapy. Br J Biomed Sci 2007;64(1):44-9.
5. Leon OS, Menendez S, Merino N, Castillo R, Sam S, Perez L, Cruz E, Bocci V. Ozone oxidative preconditioning: a protection against cellular damage by free radicals. Mediators Inflamm 1998;7(4):289-94.
6. Al-Dalain SM, Martinez G, Candelario-Jalil E, Menendez S, Re L, Giuliani A, Leon OS. Ozone treatment reduces markers of oxidative and endothelial damage in an experimental diabetes model in rats. Pharmacol Res 2001 November;44(5):391-6.
7. Ajamieh HH, Menendez S, Martinez-Sanchez G, Candelario-Jalil E, Re L, Giuliani A, Fernandez OS. Effects of ozone oxidative preconditioning on nitric oxide generation and cellular redox balance in a rat model of hepatic ischaemia-reperfusion. Liver Int 2004 February;24(1):55-62.
8. Borrego A, Zamora ZB, Gonzalez R, Romay C, Menendez S, Hernandez F, Montero T, Rojas E. Protection by ozone preconditioning is mediated by the antioxidant system in cisplatin-induced nephrotoxicity in rats. Mediators Inflamm 2004 February;13(1):13-9.
9. Zamora ZB, Borrego A, Lopez OY, Delgado R, Gonzalez R, Menendez S, Hernandez F, Schulz S. Effects of ozone oxidative preconditioning on TNF-alpha release and antioxidant-prooxidant intracellular balance in mice during endotoxic shock. Mediators Inflamm 2005 February 24;2005(1):16-22.

10. Ajamieh HH, Berlanga J, Merino N, Sanchez GM, Carmona AM, Cepero SM, Giuliani A, Re L, Leon OS. Role of protein synthesis in the protection conferred by ozone-oxidative-preconditioning in hepatic ischaemia/reperfusion. Transpl Int 2005 May;18(5):604-12.

11. Bocci V, Aldinucci C, Mosci F, Carraro F, Valacchi G. Ozonation of human blood induces a remarkable upregulation of heme oxygenase-1 and heat stress protein-70. Mediators Inflamm 2007;2007:26785.

12. Bocci V, Valacchi G, Corradeschi F, Aldinucci C, Silvestri S, Paccagnini E, Gerli R. Studies on the biological effects of ozone: 7. Generation of reactive oxygen species (ROS) after exposure of human blood to ozone. J Biol Regul Homeost Agents 1998 July;12(3):67-75.

13. Clavo B, Perez JL, Lopez L, Suarez G, Lloret M, Rodriguez V, Macias D, Santana M, Hernandez MA, Martin-Oliva R, Robaina F. Ozone Therapy for Tumor Oxygenation: a Pilot Study. Evid Based Complement Alternat Med 2004 June 1;1(1):93-8.

14. Wentworth P, Jr., McDunn JE, Wentworth AD, Takeuchi C, Nieva J, Jones T, Bautista C, Ruedi JM, Gutierrez A, Janda KD, Babior BM, Eschenmoser A, Lerner RA. Evidence for antibody-catalyzed ozone formation in bacterial killing and inflammation. Science 2002 December 13;298(5601):2195-9.

Chapter 5

1. Bradbury, R. (1953). Fahrenheit 451. New York: Ballentine Books.

2. Beckman, R.A. & Loeb , L.A. (2005). Genetic instability in cancer: Theory and experiment. Seminars in Cancer Biology, 15:423–435.

3. Sherratt, J.A. & Nowak M.A. (1992). Oncogenes, anti-oncogenes and the immune response to cancer. Biological Sciences / The Royal Society, 248(1323):261-271.

4. R. B. Scott. (1970). Cancer chemotherapy: the first twenty-five years. British Medical Journal. 4 (5730): 259–265.

5. Nixon, R. (1971). State of the Union Address. Retrieved from Internet December 12, 2008. http://www.freeinfosociety.com/media.php?id=166

6. Wyngaarden, J. B. (1988). Cecil Textbook of Medicine. Elsevier Health Sciences:

7. Abel, U. (1990). The Chemotherapy of Advanced Epithelial Cancers. Stuttgart: Hippokrates Verlag

8. Braverman, A. Medical Oncology in the 90s. The Lancet, April 13, 1991, (337) p 901

9. Bailar III, J. C. & Smith, E.M. (1986). Progress Against Cancer? New England Journal of Medicine, 314:1226-32.

10. Bailar III, J. C., Medical Uses of Statistics

11. Broder, S. (1991). Progress and challenges in the global effort against cancer. Journal of Cancer Research and Clinical Oncology, 4 (117) 290-294.

12. NCI's CancerNet Web. Retrieved from Internet, December 12, 2008. http://cancerweb.ncl.ac.uk/cancernet/600021.html

13. American Cancer Society. Cancer Facts & Figures. Retrieved from Internet December 12, 2008. http://www.cancer.org

14. Center For Disease Control. (2006). Surveillance, Epidemiology, and End Results Program, 1975-2000, Division of Cancer Control and Population Sciences.

15. Mead, G.M. Chemotherapy for solid tumours: Routine treatment not yet justified. British Medical Journal. January 28, 1995, 310(6974) 246–247.

16. Waugh, N. Health technology assessment in cancer: A personal view from public health. European Journal of Cancer, 42 (17) 2876 – 2880.

17. Dickson, M. (2004). The Cost of New Drug Discovery and Development. Discovery Medicine, 4 (22) 177.

18. Moss, R. (1995). Questioning Chemotherapy. Equinox Press.

19. Leaf, C. Why We're Losing The War On Cancer. Fortune Magazine, March 22, 2004.

20. Bailer III, J.C. & Gornik, H. L. (1997). Cancer Undefeated. New England Journal of Medicine, 22 (336) 1569-1574.

Chapter 6

1. Suh J, Rabson AB. NF-kappaB activation in human prostate cancer: important mediator or epiphenomenon? J Cell Biochem 2004 January 1;91(1):100-17.

2. Sclabas GM, Fujioka S, Schmidt C, Evans DB, Chiao PJ. NF-kappaB in pancreatic cancer. Int J Gastrointest Cancer 2003;33(1):15-26.

3. Chang AA, Van Waes C. Nuclear factor-KappaB as a common target and activator of oncogenes in head and neck squamous cell carcinoma. Adv Otorhinolaryngol 2005;62:92-102.

4. Wu JT, Kral JG. The NF-kappaB/IkappaB signaling system: a molecular target in breast cancer therapy. J Surg Res 2005 January;123(1):158-69.

5. Yu YY, Li Q, Zhu ZG. NF-kappaB as a molecular target in adjuvant therapy of gastrointestinal carcinomas. Eur J Surg Oncol 2005 May;31(4):386-92.

6. Takada Y, Murakami A, Aggarwal BB. Zerumbone abolishes NF-kappaB and IkappaBalpha kinase activation leading to suppression of antiapoptotic and metastatic gene expression, upregulation of apoptosis, and downregulation of invasion. Oncogene 2005 June 27.

7. Bentires-Alj M, Barbu V, Fillet M, Chariot A, Relic B, Jacobs N, Gielen J, Merville MP, Bours V. NF-kappaB transcription factor induces drug resistance through MDR1 expression in cancer cells. Oncogene 2003 January 9; 22(1):90-7.

8. Arlt A, Vorndamm J, Breitenbroich M, Folsch UR, Kalthoff H, Schmidt WE, Schafer H. Inhibition of NF-kappaB sensitizes human pancreatic carcinoma cells to apoptosis induced by etoposide (VP16) or doxorubicin. Oncogene 2001 February 15; 20(7):859-68.

9. Arlt A, Schafer H. NFkappaB-dependent chemoresistance in solid tumors. Int J Clin Pharmacol Ther 2002 August; 40(8):336-47.

10. Jung M, Dritschilo A. NF-kappa B signaling pathway as a target for human tumor radiosensitization. Semin Radiat Oncol 2001 October;11(4):346-51.

11. Nakanishi C, Toi M. Nuclear factor-kappaB inhibitors as sensitizers to anticancer drugs. Nat Rev Cancer 2005 April;5(4):297-309.

12. Huang S, Robinson JB, Deguzman A, Bucana CD, Fidler IJ. Blockade of nuclear factor-kappaB signaling inhibits angiogenesis and tumorigenicity of human ovarian cancer cells by suppressing expression of vascular endothelial growth factor and interleukin 8. Cancer Res 2000 October 1;60(19):5334-9.

13. Tisdale MJ. Cancer cachexia. Langenbecks Arch Surg 2004 August;389(4):299-305.

14. Chell S, Kaidi A, Williams AC, Paraskeva C. Mediators of PGE2 synthesis and signalling downstream of COX-2 represent potential targets for the prevention/treatment of colorectal cancer. Biochim Biophys Acta 2006 August;1766(1):104-19.

15. Sminia P, Kuipers G, Geldof A, Lafleur V, Slotman B. COX-2 inhibitors act as radiosensitizer in tumor treatment. Biomed Pharmacother 2005 October;59 Suppl 2:S272-S275.

16. Meric JB, Rottey S, Olaussen K, Soria JC, Khayat D, Rixe O, Spano JP. Cyclooxygenase-2 as a target for anticancer drug development. Crit Rev Oncol Hematol 2006 July;59(1):51-64.

17. Nie D. Cyclooxygenases and lipoxygenases in prostate and breast cancers. Front Biosci 2007;12:1574-85.

18. Eisinger AL, Prescott SM, Jones DA, Stafforini DM. The role of cyclooxygenase-2 and prostaglandins in colon cancer. Prostaglandins Other Lipid Mediat 2007 January;82(1-4):147-54.

19. Liao Z, Mason KA, Milas L. Cyclo-oxygenase-2 and its inhibition in cancer: is there a role? Drugs 2007;67(6):821-45.

20. Zeddou M, Greimers R, de VN, Nayjib B, Tasken K, Boniver J, Moutschen M, Rahmouni S. Prostaglandin E2 induces the expression of functional inhibitory CD94/ NKG2A receptors in human CD8+ T lymphocytes by a cAMP-dependent protein kinase A type I pathway. Biochem Pharmacol 2005 September 1;70(5):714-24.

21. Klein S, de Fougerolles AR, Blaikie P, Khan L, Pepe A, Green CD, Koteliansky V, Giancotti FG. Alpha 5 beta 1 integrin activates an NF-kappa B-dependent program of gene expression important for angiogenesis and inflammation. Mol Cell Biol 2002 August;22(16):5912-22.

22. Gately S, Li WW. Multiple roles of COX-2 in tumor angiogenesis: a target for antiangiogenic therapy. Semin Oncol 2004 April;31(2 Suppl 7):2-11.

23. Williams CS, Tsujii M, Reese J, Dey SK, DuBois RN. Host cyclooxygenase-2 modulates carcinoma growth. J Clin Invest 2000 June;105(11):1589-94.

24. Ghosh J, Myers CE. Inhibition of arachidonate 5-lipoxygenase triggers massive apoptosis in human prostate cancer cells. Proc Natl Acad Sci U S A 1998 October 27;95(22):13182-7.

25. Ding XZ, Tong WG, Adrian TE. Multiple signal pathways are involved in the mitogenic effect of 5(S)-HETE in human pancreatic cancer. Oncology 2003;65(4):285-94.

26. Ihara A, Wada K, Yoneda M, Fujisawa N, Takahashi H, Nakajima A. Blockade of leukotriene B4 signaling pathway induces apoptosis and suppresses cell proliferation in colon cancer. J Pharmacol Sci 2007 January;103(1):24-32.

27. Tong WG, Ding XZ, Witt RC, Adrian TE. Lipoxygenase inhibitors attenuate growth of human pancreatic cancer xenografts and induce apoptosis through the mitochondrial pathway. Mol Cancer Ther 2002 September;1(11):929-35.

28. Tsukada T, Nakashima K, Shirakawa S. Arachidonate 5-lipoxygenase inhibitors show potent antiproliferative effects on human leukemia cell lines. Biochem Biophys Res Commun 1986 November 14;140(3):832-6.

29. Ghosh J, Myers CE. Arachidonic acid stimulates prostate cancer cell growth: critical role of 5-lipoxygenase. Biochem Biophys Res Commun 1997 June 18;235(2):418-23.

30. Avis I, Hong SH, Martinez A, Moody T, Choi YH, Trepel J, Das R, Jett M, Mulshine JL. Five-lipoxygenase inhibitors can mediate apoptosis in human breast cancer cell lines through complex eicosanoid interactions. FASEB J 2001 September;15(11):2007-9.

31. Fan XM, Tu SP, Lam SK, Wang WP, Wu J, Wong WM, Yuen MF, Lin MC, Kung HF, Wong BC. Five-lipoxygenase-activating protein inhibitor MK-886 induces apoptosis in gastric cancer through upregulation of p27kip1 and bax. J Gastroenterol Hepatol 2004 January;19(1):31-7.

32. Hoque A, Lippman SM, Wu TT, Xu Y, Liang ZD, Swisher S, Zhang H, Cao L, Ajani JA, Xu XC. Increased 5-lipoxygenase expression and induction of apoptosis by its inhibitors in esophageal cancer: a potential target for prevention. Carcinogenesis 2005 April;26(4):785-91.

33. Matsuyama M, Yoshimura R, Mitsuhashi M, Tsuchida K, Takemoto Y, Kawahito Y, Sano H, Nakatani T. 5-Lipoxygenase inhibitors attenuate growth of human renal cell carcinoma and induce apoptosis through arachidonic acid pathway. Oncol Rep 2005 July;14(1):73-9.

34. Hayashi T, Nishiyama K, Shirahama T. Inhibition of 5-lipoxygenase pathway suppresses the growth of bladder cancer cells. Int J Urol 2006 August;13(8):1086-91.

35. Rose DP, Connolly JM, Liu XH. Fatty acid regulation of breast cancer cell growth and invasion. Adv Exp Med Biol 1997;422:47-55.

36. Hardman WE. (n-3) fatty acids and cancer therapy. J Nutr 2004 December;134(12 Suppl):3427S-30S.

37. Wen B, Deutsch E, Opolon P, Auperin A, Frascogna V, Connault E, Bourhis J. n-3 polyunsaturated fatty acids decrease mucosal/epidermal reactions and enhance antitumour effect of ionising radiation with inhibition of tumour angiogenesis. Br J Cancer 2003 September 15;89(6):1102-7.

38. Hardman WE, Sun L, Short N, Cameron IL. Dietary omega-3 fatty acids and ionizing irradiation on human breast cancer xenograft growth and angiogenesis. Cancer Cell Int 2005 April 28;5(1):12.

39. McCarty MF. Fish oil may impede tumour angiogenesis and invasiveness by down-regulating protein kinase C and modulating eicosanoid production. Med Hypotheses 1996 February;46(2):107-15.

40. Rose DP, Connolly JM. Regulation of tumor angiogenesis by dietary fatty acids and eicosanoids. Nutr Cancer 2000;37(2):119-27.

41. Murota SI, Onodera M, Morita I. Regulation of angiogenesis by controlling VEGF receptor. Ann N Y Acad Sci 2000 May;902:208-12.

42. Shtivelband MI, Juneja HS, Lee S, Wu KK. Aspirin and salicylate inhibit colon cancer medium- and VEGF-induced endothelial tube formation: correlation with suppression of cyclooxygenase-2 expression. J Thromb Haemost 2003 October;1(10):2225-33.

43. Tisdale MJ. Wasting in cancer. J Nutr 1999 January;129(1S Suppl):243S-6S.

44. Whitehouse AS, Smith HJ, Drake JL, Tisdale MJ. Mechanism of attenuation of skeletal muscle protein catabolism in cancer cachexia by eicosapentaenoic acid. Cancer Res 2001 May 1;61(9):3604-9.

45. Wigmore SJ, Barber MD, Ross JA, Tisdale MJ, Fearon KC. Effect of oral eicosapentaenoic acid on weight loss in patients with pancreatic cancer. Nutr Cancer 2000;36(2):177-84.

46. Fearon KC, von Meyenfeldt MF, Moses AG, Van Geenen R, Roy A, Gouma DJ, Giacosa A, Van Gossum A, Bauer J, Barber MD, Aaronson NK, Voss AC, Tisdale MJ. Effect of a protein and energy dense N-3 fatty acid enriched oral supplement on loss of weight and lean tissue in cancer cachexia: a randomised double blind trial. Gut 2003 October;52(10):1479-86.

47. Zi X, Agarwal R. Silibinin decreases prostate-specific antigen with cell growth inhibition via G1 arrest, leading to differentiation of prostate carcinoma cells: implications for prostate cancer intervention. Proc Natl Acad Sci U S A 1999 June 22;96(13):7490-5.

48. Kang SN, Lee MH, Kim KM, Cho D, Kim TS. Induction of human promyelocytic leukemia HL-60 cell differentiation into monocytes by silibinin: involvement of protein kinase C. Biochem Pharmacol 2001 June 15;61(12):1487-95.

49. Sharma G, Singh RP, Chan DC, Agarwal R. Silibinin induces growth inhibition and apoptotic cell death in human lung carcinoma cells. Anticancer Res 2003 May;23(3B):2649-55.

50. Qi L, Singh RP, Lu Y, Agarwal R, Harrison GS, Franzusoff A, Glode LM. Epidermal growth factor receptor mediates silibinin-induced cytotoxicity in a rat glioma cell line. Cancer Biol Ther 2003 September;2(5):526-31.

51. Agarwal C, Singh RP, Dhanalakshmi S, Tyagi AK, Tecklenburg M, Sclafani RA, Agarwal R. Silibinin upregulates the expression of cyclin-dependent kinase inhibitors and causes cell cycle arrest and apoptosis in human colon carcinoma HT-29 cells. Oncogene 2003 November 13;22(51):8271-82.

52. Tyagi AK, Agarwal C, Singh RP, Shroyer KR, Glode LM, Agarwal R. Silibinin down-regulates survivin protein and mRNA expression and causes caspases activation and apoptosis in human bladder transitional-cell papilloma RT4 cells. Biochem Biophys Res Commun 2003 December 26;312(4):1178-84.

53. Varghese L, Agarwal C, Tyagi A, Singh RP, Agarwal R. Silibinin efficacy against human hepatocellular carcinoma. Clin Cancer Res 2005 December 1;11(23):8441-8.

54. Lee SO, Jeong YJ, Im HG, Kim CH, Chang YC, Lee IS. Silibinin suppresses PMA-induced MMP-9 expression by blocking the AP-1 activation via MAPK signaling pathways in MCF-7 human breast carcinoma cells. Biochem Biophys Res Commun 2007 March 2;354(1):165-71.

55. Tyagi AK, Agarwal C, Chan DC, Agarwal R. Synergistic anti-cancer effects of silibinin with conventional cytotoxic agents doxorubicin, cisplatin and carboplatin against human breast carcinoma MCF-7 and MDA-MB468 cells. Oncol Rep 2004 February;11(2):493-9.

56. Singh RP, Agarwal R. A cancer chemopreventive agent silibinin, targets mitogenic and survival signaling in prostate cancer. Mutat Res 2004 November 2;555(1-2):21-32.

57. Hannay JA, Yu D. Silibinin: a thorny therapeutic for EGF-R expressing tumors? Cancer Biol Ther 2003 September;2(5):532-3.

58. Singh RP, Dhanalakshmi S, Tyagi AK, Chan DC, Agarwal C, Agarwal R. Dietary feeding of silibinin inhibits advance human prostate carcinoma growth in athymic nude mice and increases plasma insulin-like growth factor-binding protein-3 levels. Cancer Res 2002 June 1;62(11):3063-9.

59. Singh RP, Sharma G, Dhanalakshmi S, Agarwal C, Agarwal R. Suppression of advanced human prostate tumor growth in athymic mice by silibinin feeding is associated with reduced cell proliferation, increased apoptosis, and inhibition of angiogenesis. Cancer Epidemiol Biomarkers Prev 2003 September;12(9):933-9.

60. Gallo D, Giacomelli S, Ferlini C, Raspaglio G, Apollonio P, Prislei S, Riva A, Morazzoni P, Bombardelli E, Scambia G. Antitumour activity of the silybin-phosphatidylcholine complex, IdB 1016, against human ovarian cancer. Eur J Cancer 2003 November;39(16):2403-10.

61. Singh RP, Dhanalakshmi S, Agarwal C, Agarwal R. Silibinin strongly inhibits growth and survival of human endothelial cells via cell cycle arrest and downregulation of survivin, Akt and NF-kappaB: implications for angioprevention and antiangiogenic therapy. Oncogene 2005 February 10;24(7):1188-202.

62. Yang SH, Lin JK, Chen WS, Chiu JH. Anti-angiogenic effect of silymarin on colon cancer LoVo cell line. J Surg Res 2003 July;113(1):133-8.

63. Cao Y, Cao R. Angiogenesis inhibited by drinking tea. Nature 1999 April 1;398(6726):381.

64. Jung YD, Kim MS, Shin BA, Chay KO, Ahn BW, Liu W, Bucana CD, Gallick GE, Ellis LM. EGCG, a major component of green tea, inhibits tumour growth by inhibiting VEGF induction in human colon carcinoma cells. Br J Cancer JID - 0370635 2001 March 23;84(6):844-50.

65. Pisters KM, Newman RA, Coldman B, Shin DM, Khuri FR, Hong WK, Glisson BS, Lee JS. Phase I trial of oral green tea extract in adult patients with solid tumors. J Clin Oncol 2001 March 15;19(6):1830-8.

66. Lamy S, Gingras D, Beliveau R. Green tea catechins inhibit vascular endothelial growth factor receptor phosphorylation. Cancer Res 2002 January 15;62(2):381-5.

67. Ammon HP. Boswellic acids in chronic inflammatory diseases. Planta Med 2006 October;72(12):1100-16.

68. Catalano A, Caprari P, Soddu S, Procopio A, Romano M. 5-lipoxygenase antagonizes genotoxic stress-induced apoptosis by altering p53 nuclear trafficking. FASEB J 2004 November;18(14):1740-2.

69. Wenger FA, Kilian M, Bisevac M, Khodadayan C, von Seebach M, Schimke I, Guski H, Muller JM. Effects of Celebrex and Zyflo on liver metastasis and lipidperoxidation in pancreatic cancer in Syrian hamsters. Clin Exp Metastasis 2002;19(8):681-7.

70. Liu JJ, Nilsson A, Oredsson S, Badmaev V, Zhao WZ, Duan RD. Boswellic acids trigger apoptosis via a pathway dependent on caspase-8 activation but independent on Fas/Fas ligand interaction in colon cancer HT-29 cells. Carcinogenesis 2002 December;23(12):2087-93.

71. Zhao W, Entschladen F, Liu H, Niggemann B, Fang Q, Zaenker KS, Han R. Boswellic acid acetate induces differentiation and apoptosis in highly metastatic melanoma and fibrosarcoma cells. Cancer Detect Prev 2003;27(1):67-75.

72. Syrovets T, Gschwend JE, Buchele B, Laumonnier Y, Zugmaier W, Genze F, Simmet T. Inhibition of IkappaB kinase activity by acetyl-boswellic acids promotes apoptosis in androgen-independent PC-3 prostate cancer cells in vitro and in vivo. J Biol Chem 2005 February 18;280(7):6170-80.

73. Xia L, Chen D, Han R, Fang Q, Waxman S, Jing Y. Boswellic acid acetate induces apoptosis through caspase-mediated pathways in myeloid leukemia cells. Mol Cancer Ther 2005 March;4(3):381-8.

74. Liu JJ, Huang B, Hooi SC. Acetyl-keto-beta-boswellic acid inhibits cellular proliferation through a p21-dependent pathway in colon cancer cells. Br J Pharmacol 2006 August;148(8):1099-107.

75. Janssen G, Bode U, Breu H, Dohrn B, Engelbrecht V, Gobel U. Boswellic acids in the palliative therapy of children with progressive or relapsed brain tumors. Klin Padiatr 2000 July;212(4):189-95.

76. Streffer JR, Bitzer M, Schabet M, Dichgans J, Weller M. Response of radiochemotherapy-associated cerebral edema to a phytotherapeutic agent, H15. Neurology 2001 May 8;56(9):1219-21.

77. Winking M, Sarikaya S, Rahmanian A, Jodicke A, Boker DK. Boswellic acids inhibit glioma growth: a new treatment option? J Neurooncol 2000;46(2):97-103.

78. Whittle BJ, Hansen D, Salmon JA. Gastric ulcer formation and cyclo-oxygenase inhibition in cat antrum follows parenteral administration of aspirin but not salicylate. Eur J Pharmacol 1985 October 8;116(1-2):153-7.

79. Zambraski EJ, Atkinson DC, Diamond J. Effects of salicylate vs. aspirin on renal prostaglandins and function in normal and sodium-depleted dogs. J Pharmacol Exp Ther 1988 October;247(1):96-103.

80. Cryer B, Goldschmiedt M, Redfern JS, Feldman M. Comparison of salsalate and aspirin on mucosal injury and gastroduodenal mucosal prostaglandins. Gastroenterology 1990 December;99(6):1616-21.

81. Kopp E, Ghosh S. Inhibition of NF-kappa B by sodium salicylate and aspirin. Science 1994 August 12;265(5174):956-9.

82. Yin MJ, Yamamoto Y, Gaynor RB. The anti-inflammatory agents aspirin and salicylate inhibit the activity of I(kappa)B kinase-beta. Nature 1998 November 5;396(6706):77-80.

83. Borthwick GM, Johnson AS, Partington M, Burn J, Wilson R, Arthur HM. Therapeutic levels of aspirin and salicylate directly inhibit a model of angiogenesis through a Cox-independent mechanism. FASEB J 2006 October;20(12):2009-16.

84. McCarty MF, Block KI. Preadministration of high-dose salicylates, suppressors of NF-kappaB activation, may increase the chemosensitivity of many cancers: an example of proapoptotic signal modulation therapy. Integr Cancer Ther 2006 September;5(3):252-68.

85. McCarty MF, Block KI. Toward a core nutraceutical program for cancer management. Integr Cancer Ther 2006 June;5(2):150-71.

86. McPherson TC. Salsalate for arthritis: a clinical evaluation. Clin Ther 1984;6(4):388-403.

87. Boettcher FA, Salvi RJ. Salicylate ototoxicity: review and synthesis. Am J Otolaryngol 1991 January;12(1):33-47.

88. Cryer B, Feldman M. Cyclooxygenase-1 and cyclooxygenase-2 selectivity of widely used nonsteroidal anti-inflammatory drugs. Am J Med 1998 May;104(5):413-21.

89. Van HA, Schwartz JI, Depre M, de L, I, Dallob A, Tanaka W, Wynants K, Buntinx A, Arnout J, Wong PH, Ebel DL, Gertz BJ, De Schepper PJ. Comparative inhibitory activity of rofecoxib, meloxicam, diclofenac, ibuprofen, and naproxen on COX-2 versus COX-1 in healthy volunteers. J Clin Pharmacol 2000 October;40(10):1109-20.

90. Jick SS, Kaye JA, Jick H. Diclofenac and acute myocardial infarction in patients with no major risk factors. Br J Clin Pharmacol 2007 November;64(5):662-7.

91. Lovborg H, Oberg F, Rickardson L, Gullbo J, Nygren P, Larsson R. Inhibition of proteasome activity, nuclear factor-KappaB translocation and cell survival by the antialcoholism drug disulfiram. Int J Cancer 2006 March 15;118(6):1577-80.

92. Chen D, Cui QC, Yang H, Dou QP. Disulfiram, a clinically used anti-alcoholism drug and copper-binding agent, induces apoptotic cell death in breast cancer cultures and xenografts via inhibition of the proteasome activity. Cancer Res 2006 November 1;66(21):10425-33.

93. Zavrski I, Kleeberg L, Kaiser M, Fleissner C, Heider U, Sterz J, Jakob C, Sezer O. Proteasome as an emerging therapeutic target in cancer. Curr Pharm Des 2007;13(5):471-85.

Chapter 7

1. Sun Y. Free radicals, antioxidant enzymes, and carcinogenesis. Free Radic Biol Med 1990;8(6):583-99.

2. Kwei KA, Finch JS, Thompson EJ, Bowden GT. Transcriptional repression of catalase in mouse skin tumor progression. Neoplasia 2004 September;6(5):440-8.

3. Tas F, Hansel H, Belce A, Ilvan S, Argon A, Camlica H, Topuz E. Oxidative stress in breast cancer. Med Oncol 2005;22(1):11-5.

4. Arnold RS, Shi J, Murad E, Whalen AM, Sun CQ, Polavarapu R, Parthasarathy S, Petros JA, Lambeth JD. Hydrogen peroxide mediates the cell growth and transformation caused by the mitogenic oxidase Nox1. Proc Natl Acad Sci U S A 2001 May 8;98(10):5550-5.

5. Vaquero EC, Edderkaoui M, Pandol SJ, Gukovsky I, Gukovskaya AS. Reactive oxygen species produced by NAD(P)H oxidase inhibit apoptosis in pancreatic cancer cells. J Biol Chem 2004 August 13;279(33):34643-54.

6. Lim SD, Sun C, Lambeth JD, Marshall F, Amin M, Chung L, Petros JA, Arnold RS. Increased Nox1 and hydrogen peroxide in prostate cancer. Prostate 2005 February 1;62(2):200-7.

7. Arnold RS, Shi J, Murad E, Whalen AM, Sun CQ, Polavarapu R, Parthasarathy S, Petros JA, Lambeth JD. Hydrogen peroxide mediates the cell growth and transformation caused by the mitogenic oxidase Nox1. Proc Natl Acad Sci U S A 2001 May 8;98(10):5550-5.

8. Chen Q, Espey MG, Krishna MC, Mitchell JB, Corpe CP, Buettner GR, Shacter E, Levine M. Pharmacologic ascorbic acid concentrations selectively kill cancer cells: action as a pro-drug to deliver hydrogen peroxide to tissues. Proc Natl Acad Sci U S A 2005 September 20;102(38):13604-9.

9. Chen Q, Espey MG, Sun AY, Lee JH, Krishna MC, Shacter E, Choyke PL, Pooput C, Kirk KL, Buettner GR, Levine M. Ascorbate in pharmacologic concentrations selectively generates ascorbate radical and hydrogen peroxide in extracellular fluid in vivo. Proc Natl Acad Sci U S A 2007 May 22;104(21):8749-54.

10. Padayatty SJ, Sun H, Wang Y, Riordan HD, Hewitt SM, Katz A, Wesley RA, Levine M. Vitamin C pharmacokinetics: implications for oral and intravenous use. Ann Intern Med 2004 April 6;140(7):533-7.

11. Padayatty SJ, Levine M. Reevaluation of ascorbate in cancer treatment: emerging evidence, open minds and serendipity. J Am Coll Nutr 2000 August;19(4):423-5.

12. Riordan HD, Casciari JJ, Gonzalez MJ, Riordan NH, Miranda-Massari JR, Taylor P, Jackson JA. A pilot clinical study of continuous intravenous ascorbate in terminal cancer patients. P R Health Sci J 2005 December;24(4):269-76.

13. Padayatty SJ, Riordan HD, Hewitt SM, Katz A, Hoffer LJ, Levine M. Intravenously administered vitamin C as cancer therapy: three cases. CMAJ 2006 March 28;174(7):937-42.

14. Calderon PB, Cadrobbi J, Marques C, Hong-Ngoc N, Jamison JM, Gilloteaux J, Summers JL, Taper HS. Potential therapeutic application of the association of vitamins C and K3 in cancer treatment. Curr Med Chem 2002 December;9(24):2271-85.

15. Verrax J, Stockis J, Tison A, Taper HS, Calderon PB. Oxidative stress by ascorbate/menadione association kills K562 human chronic myelogenous leukaemia cells and inhibits its tumour growth in nude mice. Biochem Pharmacol 2006 September 14;72(6):671-80.

16. Taper HS, Jamison JM, Gilloteaux J, Summers JL, Calderon PB. Inhibition of the development of metastases by dietary vitamin C:K3 combination. Life Sci 2004 July 9;75(8):955-67.

17. Tetef M, Margolin K, Ahn C, Akman S, Chow W, Coluzzi P, Leong L, Morgan RJ, Jr., Raschko J, Shibata S, . Mitomycin C and menadione for the treatment of advanced gastrointestinal cancers: a phase II trial. J Cancer Res Clin Oncol 1995;121(2):103-6.

18. Tetef M, Margolin K, Ahn C, Akman S, Chow W, Leong L, Morgan RJ, Jr., Raschko J, Somlo G, Doroshow JH. Mitomycin C and menadione for the treatment of lung cancer: a phase II trial. Invest New Drugs 1995;13(2):157-62.

Chapter 8

1.Cat Facts. Cat Scans. Retrieved from Internet, September 19, 2008. http://www.catscans.com/facts.htm

2. Wikipedia. Immune System.   Retrieved from Internet, July 14, 2008. http://en.wikipedia.org/wiki/Immune_system

3. Lissoni P. Is there a role for melatonin in supportive care? Support Care Cancer 2002;10(2):110-6.

4. Lissoni P, Barni S, Mandala M, Ardizzoia A, Paolorossi F, Vaghi M, Longarini R, Malugani F, Tancini G. Decreased toxicity and increased efficacy of cancer chemotherapy using the pineal hormone melatonin in metastatic solid tumour patients with poor clinical status. Eur J Cancer 1999;35(12):1688-92.

5. Lissoni P. Biochemotherapy with standard chemotherapies plus the pineal hormone melatonin in the treatment of advanced solid neoplasms. Pathol Biol (Paris) 2007;55(3-4):201-4.

6. Nunnari G, Nigro L, Palermo F, Leto D, Pomerantz RJ, Cacopardo B. Reduction of serum melatonin levels in HIV-1-infected individuals' parallel disease progression: correlation with serum interleukin-12 levels. Infection 2003;31(6):379-82.

7. Miller G, Lahrs S, Dematteo RP. Overexpression of interleukin-12 enables dendritic cells to activate NK cells and confer systemic antitumor immunity. FASEB J 2003;17(6):728-30.

8. Del VM, Bajetta E, Canova S, Lotze MT, Wesa A, Parmiani G, Anichini A. Interleukin-12: biological properties and clinical application. Clin Cancer Res 2007;13(16):4677-85.

9. Koizumi SI, Wakita D, Sato T, Mitamura R, Izumo T, Shibata H, Kiso Y, Chamoto K, Togashi Y, Kitamura H, Nishimura T. Essential role of Toll-like receptors for dendritic cell and NK1.1(+) cell-dependent activation of type 1 immunity by Lactobacillus pentosus strain S-PT84. Immunol Lett 2008 July 11.

10. Mohamadzadeh M, Olson S, Kalina WV, Ruthel G, Demmin GL, Warfield KL, Bavari S, Klaenhammer TR. Lactobacilli activate human dendritic cells that skew T cells toward T helper 1 polarization. Proc Natl Acad Sci U S A 2005;102(8):2880-5.

11. Hoarau C, Lagaraine C, Martin L, Velge-Roussel F, Lebranchu Y. Supernatant of Bifidobacterium breve induces dendritic cell maturation, activation, and survival through a Toll-like receptor 2 pathway. J Allergy Clin Immunol 2006;117(3):696-702.

12. Roy M, Kiremidjian-Schumacher L, Wishe HI, Cohen MW, Stotzky G. Supplementation with selenium and human immune cell functions. I. Effect on lymphocyte proliferation and interleukin 2 receptor expression. Biol Trace Elem Res 1994;41(1-2):103-14.

13. Kiremidjian-Schumacher L, Roy M, Wishe HI, Cohen MW, Stotzky G. Supplementation with selenium and human immune cell functions. II. Effect on cytotoxic lymphocytes and natural killer cells. Biol Trace Elem Res 1994;41(1-2):115-27.

14. Kiremidjian-Schumacher L, Roy M, Wishe HI, Cohen MW, Stotzky G. Supplementation with selenium augments the functions of natural killer and lymphokine-activated killer cells. Biol Trace Elem Res 1996;52(3):227-39.

15. Kikuchi Y, Oomori K, Kizawa I, Kato K. Augmented natural killer activity in ovarian cancer patients treated with cimetidine. Eur J Cancer Clin Oncol 1986;22(9):1037-43.

16. Allen JI, Syropoulos HJ, Grant B, Eagon JC, Kay NE. Cimetidine modulates natural killer cell function of patients with chronic lymphocytic leukemia. J Lab Clin Med 1987;109(4):396-401.

17. Kubota T, Fujiwara H, Ueda Y, Itoh T, Yamashita T, Yoshimura T, Okugawa K, Yamamoto Y, Yano Y, Yamagishi H. Cimetidine modulates the antigen presenting capacity of dendritic cells from colorectal cancer patients. Br J Cancer 2002;86(8):1257-61.

18. Ghiringhelli F, Menard C, Puig PE, Ladoire S, Roux S, Martin F, Solary E, Le CA, Zitvogel L, Chauffert B. Metronomic cyclophosphamide regimen selectively depletes CD4+CD25+ regulatory T cells and restores T and NK effector functions in end stage cancer patients. Cancer Immunol Immunother 2007;56(5):641-8.

19. Ohta A, Gorelik E, Prasad SJ, Ronchese F, Lukashev D, Wong MK, Huang X, Caldwell S, Liu K, Smith P, Chen JF, Jackson EK, Apasov S, Abrams S, Sitkovsky M. A2A adenosine receptor protects tumors from antitumor T cells. Proc Natl Acad Sci U S A 2006;103(35):13132-7.

20. Sitkovsky M, Lukashev D, Deaglio S, Dwyer K, Robson SC, Ohta A. Adenosine A2A receptor antagonists: blockade of adenosinergic effects and T regulatory cells. Br J Pharmacol 2008;153 Suppl 1:S457-S464.

21. Takahashi A, Hanson MG, Norell HR, Havelka AM, Kono K, Malmberg KJ, Kiessling RV. Preferential cell death of CD8+ effector memory (CCR7-CD45RA-) T cells by hydrogen peroxide-induced oxidative stress. J Immunol 2005;174(10):6080-7.
22. Betten A, Dahlgren C, Mellqvist UH, Hermodsson S, Hellstrand K. Oxygen radical-induced natural killer cell dysfunction: role of myeloperoxidase and regulation by serotonin. J Leukoc Biol 2004;75(6):1111-5.
23. Thoren FB, Romero AI, Hellstrand K. Oxygen radicals induce poly(ADP-ribose) polymerase-dependent cell death in cytotoxic lymphocytes. J Immunol 2006;176(12):7301-7.
24. Blanchetot C, Boonstra J. The ROS-NOX connection in cancer and angiogenesis. Crit Rev Eukaryot Gene Expr 2008;18(1):35-45.
25. McCarty MF, Barroso-Aranda J, Contreras F. A two-phase strategy for treatment of oxidant-dependent cancers. Med Hypotheses 2007;69(3):489-96.
26. McCarty MF. Clinical potential of Spirulina as a source of phycocyanobilin. J Med Food 2007;10(4):566-70.
27. Pugh N, Ross SA, ElSohly HN, ElSohly MA, Pasco DS. Isolation of three high molecular weight polysaccharide preparations with potent immunostimulatory activity from Spirulina platensis, aphanizomenon flos-aquae and Chlorella pyrenoidosa. Planta Med 2001;67(8):737-42.
28. Hirahashi T, Matsumoto M, Hazeki K, Saeki Y, Ui M, Seya T. Activation of the human innate immune system by Spirulina: augmentation of interferon production and NK cytotoxicity by oral administration of hot water extract of Spirulina platensis. Int Immunopharmacol 2002;2(4):423-34.
29. Ushio-Fukai M, Nakamura Y. Reactive oxygen species and angiogenesis: NADPH oxidase as target for cancer therapy. Cancer Lett 2008;266(1):37-52.

Chapter 9

1. McCarty MF. Insulin and IGF-I as determinants of low "Western" cancer rates in the rural third world. Int J Epidemiol 2004 August;33(4):908-10.
2. Giovannucci E. Nutrition, insulin, insulin-like growth factors and cancer. Horm Metab Res 2003 November;35(11-12):694-704.
3. Jousse C, Bruhat A, Ferrara M, Fafournoux P. Physiological concentration of amino acids regulates insulin-like- growth-factor-binding protein 1 expression. Biochem J 1998 August 15;334 (Pt 1):147-53.
4. Allen NE, Appleby PN, Davey GK, Key TJ. Hormones and diet: low insulin-like growth factor-I but normal bioavailable androgens in vegan men. Br J Cancer 2000 July;83(1):95-7.
5. Baserga R. The insulin-like growth factor-I receptor as a target for cancer therapy. Expert Opin Ther Targets 2005 August;9(4):753-68.
6. Ngo TH, Barnard RJ, Leung PS, Cohen P, Aronson WJ. Insulin-like growth factor I (IGF-I) and IGF binding protein-1 modulate prostate cancer cell growth and apoptosis: possible mediators for the effects of diet and exercise on cancer cell survival. Endocrinology 2003 June;144(6):2319-24.
7. Barnard RJ, Ngo TH, Leung PS, Aronson WJ, Golding LA. A low-fat diet and/or strenuous exercise alters the IGF axis in vivo and reduces prostate tumor cell growth in vitro. Prostate 2003 August 1;56(3):201-6.
8. Borugian MJ, Sheps SB, Kim-Sing C, Olivotto IA, Van Patten C, Dunn BP, Coldman AJ, Potter JD, Gallagher RP, Hislop TG. Waist-to-hip ratio and breast cancer mortality. Am J Epidemiol 2003 November 15;158(10):963-8.
9. Pasanisi P, Berrino F, De PM, Venturelli E, Mastroianni A, Panico S. Metabolic syndrome as a prognostic factor for breast cancer recurrences. Int J Cancer 2006 July 1;119(1):236-8.

10. Holmes MD, Chen WY, Feskanich D, Kroenke CH, Colditz GA. Physical activity and survival after breast cancer diagnosis. JAMA 2005 May 25;293(20):2479-86.

11. Meyerhardt JA, Heseltine D, Niedzwiecki D, Hollis D, Saltz LB, Mayer RJ, Thomas J, Nelson H, Whittom R, Hantel A, Schilsky RL, Fuchs CS. Impact of physical activity on cancer recurrence and survival in patients with stage III colon cancer: findings from CALGB 89803. J Clin Oncol 2006 August 1;24(22):3535-41.

12. Meyerhardt JA, Giovannucci EL, Holmes MD, Chan AT, Chan JA, Colditz GA, Fuchs CS. Physical activity and survival after colorectal cancer diagnosis. J Clin Oncol 2006 August 1;24(22):3527-34.

13. Hutnick NA, Williams NI, Kraemer WJ, Orsega-Smith E, Dixon RH, Bleznak AD, Mastro AM. Exercise and lymphocyte activation following chemotherapy for breast cancer. Med Sci Sports Exerc 2005 November;37(11):1827-35.

14. Quist M, Rorth M, Zacho M, Andersen C, Moeller T, Midtgaard J, Adamsen L. High-intensity resistance and cardiovascular training improve physical capacity in cancer patients undergoing chemotherapy. Scand J Med Sci Sports 2006 October;16(5):349-57.

15. Lavigne JA, Baer DJ, Wimbrow HH, Albert PS, Brown ED, Judd JT, Campbell WS, Giffen CA, Dorgan JF, Hartman TJ, Barrett JC, Hursting SD, Taylor PR. Effects of alcohol on insulin-like growth factor I and insulin-like growth factor binding protein 3 in postmenopausal women. Am J Clin Nutr 2005 February;81(2):503-7.

16. Rojdmark S, Rydvald Y, Aquilonius A, Brismar K. Insulin-like growth factor (IGF)-1 and IGF-binding protein-1 concentrations in serum of normal subjects after alcohol ingestion: evidence for decreased IGF-1 bioavailability. Clin Endocrinol (Oxf) 2000 March;52(3):313-8.

17. Farchi G, Fidanza F, Giampaoli S, Mariotti S, Menotti A. Alcohol and survival in the Italian rural cohorts of the Seven Countries Study. Int J Epidemiol 2000 August;29(4):667-71.

18. Byles J, Young A, Furuya H, Parkinson L. A drink to healthy aging: The association between older women's use of alcohol and their health-related quality of life. J Am Geriatr Soc 2006 September;54(9):1341-7.

19. Keum YS, Jeong WS, Kong AN. Chemopreventive functions of isothiocyanates. Drug News Perspect 2005 September;18(7):445-51.

20. Munday R, Munday CM. Induction of phase II enzymes by aliphatic sulfides derived from garlic and onions: an overview. Methods Enzymol 2004;382:449-56.

21. McCarty MF, Barroso-Aranda J, Contreras F. A two-phase strategy for treatment of oxidant-dependent cancers. Med Hypotheses 2007 May 12.

22. Brar SS, Kennedy TP, Quinn M, Hoidal JR. Redox signaling of NF-kappaB by membrane NAD(P)H oxidases in normal and malignant cells. Protoplasma 2003 May;221(1-2):117-27.

23. Wu WS. The signaling mechanism of ROS in tumor progression. Cancer Metastasis Rev 2006 December;25(4):695-705.

24. Pugh N, Ross SA, ElSohly HN, ElSohly MA, Pasco DS. Isolation of three high molecular weight polysaccharide preparations with potent immunostimulatory activity from Spirulina platensis, aphanizomenon flos-aquae and Chlorella pyrenoidosa. Planta Med 2001 November;67(8):737-42.

Chapter 11

1. Wallace, C. Faith and Healing. Time, 1996 June 24.

2. Benson, H. (1996). Timeless Healing. New York: Simon and Schuster.

Share The Hope

You may know someone who would benefit from reading this book. It is easy to share the hope with others. Here are three ways:

1. Suggest to your loved one to request a free copy of Hope, Medicine & Healing through our website www.oasisofhope.com. We will ship it out at no cost. You can refer people to this website and even email them the link.
2. Suggest to your friend to call us toll free at 1-888-500-HOPE to request a copy.
3. Give your copy to the person who needs it. You can always contact us and request another copy at no charge.

One of the great rewards in life is being able to sow hope in others.

Contact Oasis of Hope

  If you would like to explore the treatment options at Oasis of Hope, please contact us. You will be able to speak with one of our health advisors at no cost to you and one of our physicians will develop a personalized treatment program for you.

Oasis of Hope
Toll free from USA: 1-888-500-HOPE
Direct: 1 (619) 690-8450
Fax: 1 (619) 690-8410
Toll free from Mexico: 01-800-026-2747
Direct in Mexico: 664-631-6124
Fax in Mexico: 664-631-6154
Email: health@oasisofhope.com
www.oasisofhope.com

DVD Offer

Call or order online to receive 50% off of this DVD that explains the Oasis of Hope Integrative Regulatory Therapy. It features lectures by Dr. Francisco Contreras, Daniel E. Kennedy, Dr. Jorge Barroso-Aranda, Mark McCarty, and Leticia Wong.